The Gods
And the Demons
Are Not Two

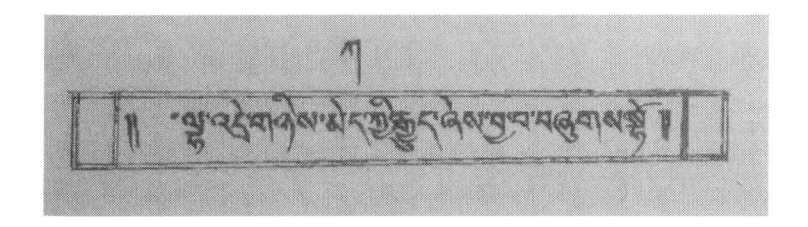

A Tantra of the Great Perfection

With Tibetan Text

Translated by

Christopher Wilkinson

Cover image: detail from a Thangka of Abhayakaragupta

Renowned as a scholar and pre-incarnation of the Panchen Lama

Silk brocade woven on the Imperial Looms at Hangchow China as an offering to the 9th Panchen Lama, Thupten Chokyi Nyima.

Collection of Moke Mokotoff, New York, NY

No part of this book may be reproduced in any form or by any electronic or mechanical means including information storage and retrieval systems, without permission in writing from the author. The only exception is by a reviewer, who may quote excerpts in a review.

Published by Christopher Wilkinson

Cambridge, MA, USA

Copyright © 2015 Christopher Wilkinson

All rights reserved.

ISBN: 1519615701
ISBN-13: 978-1519615701

DEDICATION

To the memory and inspiration of Dilgo Khyentse Rinpoche.

ALSO TRANSLATED BY CHRISTOPHER WILKINSON

Great Perfection Series:

The Tantra of Great Bliss:
The Guhyagarbha Transmission of Vajrasattva's Magnificent Sky

Secret Sky:
The Ancient Tantras on Vajrasattva's Magnificent Sky

The Great Tantra of Vajrasattva:
Equal to the End of the Sky

Beyond Secret:
The Upadesha of Vairochana on the Practice of the Great Perfection

Secret Wisdom:
Three Root Tantras of the Great Perfection

Sakya Kongma Series:

Sakya Pandita's Poetic Wisdom

Jetsun Dragpa Gyaltsan: The Hermit King

Admission at Dharma's Gate by Sonam Tsemo

An Overview of Tantra and Related Works

Chogyal Phagpa: The Emperor's Guru

Advice to Kublai Khan: Letters by the Tibetan Monk Chogyal Phagpa to Kublai Khan and his Court

CONTENTS

    Acknowledgments   i

    Introduction   iii

1   The All Good One is Beyond the Dharma   1

2   A Discourse in which Vajra Dharma Mati Blesses the Five Nirmaṇakāyas   9

3   An Explanation of the Blessings of the Three Kayas of the Children of the Victorious Ones   17

4   Self-Liberation through Recognition of the View   25

5   Recognizing the Meditator and Cutting through the Roots of Mara's Life   31

6   The Recognition of Maras in our Practice   37

7   A Presentation on Results   43

8   A Description of the Dharmakāya's Blessings upon the Sambhogakāya   55

9   A Description of the Blessings of the Dharmakāya and the Recognition of the Dharmakāya in the Six Classes of Living Things   67

10   Recognition of the Sambhogakāya   71

11   The Nirmaṇakāya appears in the Circle of the Light of Awareness   79

12   The Revelation that Vemacitra is a Nirmaṇakāya   83

13   Sharing the Taste of Being an External Fury   89

14   Sharing the Taste of Diseases from Intermittent Attachment and Hatred   95

15   Sharing a Taste for Ideas   101

16   Sharing the Taste of Being a Secret and Unsurpassed Deity   109

17	The Time of the Destruction of the World	113
18	Living in a Peaceful Abiding	117
19	Teachings on the Roots of our Attachments to the World	121
20	Attachment to the Land of the Gods and Teaching the Dharma There	125
21	Attachment to Self-originating Compassion while in the Land of the Humans	129
22	The Ways in which the Asuras are Attached, and Turning the Wheel of the Dharma for Them	133
23	The Ways we are Attached to the World of the Animals and the Descent of Compassion Even on Them	137
24	Teachings to Destroy that Hungry Ghosts' Attachment to the External World and Turning the Wheel that Brings Compassion Down from Above	141
25	Turning the Wheel of the Dharma of Compassion in the Abodes of Hell	145
26	Turning the Wheel of Self-evident Compassion for the Cold Hells and for the Temporary Hells that are Near Them	147
27	Teaching the Way We Become Attached to the Vajra Hell and Turning the Wheel of the Dharma of Compassion There	149
28	A Teaching that Turns the Wheel of the Dharma of Compassion on Attachment, Destruction, and Emptiness, along with the Three Kinds of Beings who Experience Them and That Their Magnificent Pilgrimage Sites Will Not Endure	153
29	Teaching that Compassion Falls upon the Philosophical Theories in the Scriptures about the Vehicles and their Conclusive Result	157
30	The Spike of Reason Is Planted through the External and Internal and Plants the Spike of Analogies for Teaching, Plants the Spike of Words of Vision, and Plants the Spike of Meanings into Words	161
31	Revealing the Heart that Conceals the External, Internal, and Secret	163

32	The Bequest of the Tantra	165
	Tibetan Text	167
	About the Translator	215
	Notes to the Introduction	217

ACKNOWLEDGMENTS

First and foremost, I wish to thank my root teacher Dezhung Rinpoche for constantly bringing out the best in me and encouraging me to pursue a comprehension of every branch of Buddhist learning. It was he who introduced me to Dilgo Kyentse Rinpoche, and through his recommendations enabled me to receive full empowerments, transmissions, and permissions in the areas of Mahā, Anu, and Ati Yogas. With the highest regard I wish to thank Dilgo Kyentse Rinpoche, Khetsun Zangpo Rinpoche, Nyoshul Khen Rinpoche, and Khenpo Palden Sherab for their kind instruction and encouragement in my effort to translate the literature of the rDzogs chen. There are many individuals, too many to name here, that have helped me over the years to become a qualified translator, in many ways. At this time I want to remember the kindness of Ngawang Kunga Trinlay Sakyapa, Jigdral Dagchen Sakya Rinpoche, Dhongthog Rinpoche, H.H. Karmapa Rangjung Rigpay Dorje, Kalu Rinpoche, Chogyam Trungpa Rinpoche, Geshe Ngawang Nornang, Carl Potter, David Ruegg, Turrell Wylie, Gene Smith, Karen Lang, Richard Solomon, Jack Hawley, David Jackson, Cyrus Stearns, Herbert Guenther, Eva Neumeier-Dargyay, Leslie Kawamura, Robert Thurman, Paul Nietupski, Lou Lancaster, David Snellgrove, Jean-Luc Achard, Steve Landsberg, Tsultrim Alione, Carolyn Klein, Rob Mayer, Jonathan Silk, David White, Mark Tatz, Steve Goodman, and Kennard Lipman. I want to make special thanks to Sarah Moosvi for proofing the manuscript, to Robert J. Barnhart for his generous support, and to Moke Mokotoff for the use of a detail on a thangka for the cover of this book. The many people who have contributed to my understanding and ability to do this work cannot be counted. I wish to thank everyone that has taken a kind interest in these translations, however slight, for your part in making this work a reality.

A Tantra of the Great Perfection

INTRODUCTION

To those familiar with the esoteric traditions of Buddhism, the Great Perfection is well known as a pathway of instant enlightenment, a vehicle for a sudden breakthrough of enlightened awareness here in the present. We may wonder, though, what the Great Perfection has to say about the obvious reality that there are all kinds of different beings who live under all kinds of conditions, and the reality that we ourselves go through all kinds of emotional turbulence even as we study the Great Perfection. What does the Great Perfection have to say about the demonic side of things? What does it say about our understandings of what divine beings are? How does it integrate a vision of the divine and the demonic into the fabric of instantaneous enlightenment? How do practitioners of the Great Perfection understand their own demons and preferred deities, and come to terms with them? In a world view wherein everyone is already enlightened, what is the function of compassion? These concerns are addressed in The Gods and the Demons Are Not Two.

This Tantra offers a lengthy discussion of the demonic and the divine, with information on the recognition of demons and their different classes, how we can know whether our lives are controlled by demons, a discussion of exorcism, and a thorough presentation on the Great Perfection's concern for all classes of living beings. We are introduced into a mythological world populated by a wide variety of demonic and heavenly beings and are encouraged to "share the taste" (*ro snyoms*) of what life is like for them, a kind of sympathetic comprehension of other beings. We are guided through the realms of samsara, and encouraged to share in the taste of what it would be like if we were some other being. How would it feel to be an element, a demon, an illness, a denizen of hell, an animal, or a god? Empathy is used to point us toward an understanding of a kind of perfection that there is in each and every living thing, a great perfection.

As you get into the Tantra you will see that language and translation are primary concerns. You will read of the first dissemination of these teachings by a turquoise cuckoo bird, singing in Sanskrit. The audience, speaking Tibetan, requests the teachings to be given in their own language. The bird transforms into a boy, and speaks out the teachings in a Sanskrit that everyone is supposed to understand in their own language. Then, through the rest of the Tantra, we then see the use of short Sanskrit sayings combined with Tibetan explanations of their meaning. This points to a time in the Transmission of the Dharma to Tibet when teachers from India and elsewhere would give talks in their own languages that included pithy renderings of the teachings, which were then translated into Tibetan, or where Tibetan teachers would read from a work in Sanskrit and then comment on it in Tibetan. The structure of the text lends itself to this understanding, for we find commentarial information at the endings of many of the chapters.

As readers, we are drawn into a world where incomprehensible teachers, with the help of Tibetan translators, present instructions, commenting on them with information relevant to the Tibetan audience. The situation is very much like one of an English speaker attending a teaching by a Tibetan Lama in the modern world, where a translator sits next to the teacher and tells the audience what was said and notes are later added to make a book out of the teaching. We have, then, a snapshot of the transmission of the Dharma into Tibet from around the 8th century of our era. Those interested in translation theory will find these early Tibetan insights into language and translation most interesting.

The exact dating of this work is difficult to determine. One manuscript witness is found in the *Vairo'i rGyud 'bum*,[i] the Hundred Thousand Tantras of Vairochana, which indicates that the compilers of that collection considered this Tantra to be a translation by Vairochana, a famous Tibetan translator who was active in the latter part of the 8th century of our era. In his introduction to The Marvelous Primordial State, Chogyal Namkhai Norbu indicates that the *Vairo'i rGyud 'bum* is a very old collection and demonstrates its importance in helping him determine which was the earliest Mejung Tantra.[ii] We can therefore be sure that the Tibetan tradition holds The Gods and the Demons Are Not Two to be a very ancient work. It is even possible that we have here a kind of mythical documentation of Vairochana's own efforts as a translator at the side of his teacher Śrī Singha. There is no colophon to the text, and no translator is mentioned. There are many possible reasons for this. It is not uncommon for this information to be missing from a translation. The Gods and the Demons Are Not Two was also not included in the *Kagyur*, the official canon of Buddhist works that had been translated into Tibetan, probably because it is evidently not a translation, but a Tibetan work containing translated passages. It was, however, faithfully copied over the centuries and is found today in not only the Hundred Thousand Tantras of Vairochana, but in several editions of the Nyingma Gyubum, the Hundred Thousand Tantras of the Ancients.[iii] I have used the manuscript found in the mTshams brag manuscript as primary, referring to the *Vairo'i rGyud 'bum* manuscript in cases where readings required clarification. I have included images of the mTshams brag manuscript edition at the end of this book, to help preserve this literature and for your convenience.

I have identified two companion works to The Gods and the Demons Are Not Two: The Tantra on the Revolt of the Asura Armies,[iv] and the Tantra on the Total Subjugation of the Furies.[v] These titles share the basic features of being dialogues between Vajra Dharma Mati and the All Good One and having content concerning gods, asuras, demons, and the elemental furies. Neither of these latter two titles are witnessed in the *Vairo'i rGyud 'bum*, while content that we find in both of them is to be found here in The Gods and the Demons Are Not Two. It appears then that these two titles were released after the present Tantra.

I have striven to translate in a way that is both true to the original and retains literary quality in the English. In cases where further research is desirable for technical terms, I have footnoted them. I hope you find reading this Tantra both informative and enjoyable.

Thank you.

Christopher Wilkinson
Dec. 1, 2015

THE GODS AND THE DEMONS ARE NOT TWO:

A TANTRA OF THE GREAT PERFECTION

In the Indian language:

Dewa Huṃ Ye Shes[1] Yaman Hri Bhutid Tantra Nāma

In the Tibetan language:

Lha 'dre gnyis med kyi rgyud ches bya ba

In the English language:

The Tantra on the Non-duality of the Gods and the Demons

---

[1] "Ye shes" is the word for wisdom in the Tibetan language, and is not a Sanskrit word. The insertion of a Tibetan word into the Indian language title might indicate that the Tibetan authors did not know Sanskrit well enough to fabricate a title in that language.

THE ALL GOOD ONE IS BEYOND THE DHARMA

I bow to the All Good One,
The spontaneously formed circle.[2]

It is time for me to tell you these words:

In the grounds where the gods of the good Dharma gather,
There is a place where there is a pure and open lotus.
It is in the realm of great bliss.

The All Good One,
Who is a fully perfected Buddha,
Is the foremost of teachers.
His entourage consists of five perfect Buddhas.

In the mandala of the origin of all the teachings,
There is a place that pervasively encompasses all things.

When knowledge of the core of our foundation is distorted,
Our senses illuminate themselves.
They are five mirrors.
Our convictions illuminate themselves.
They are five Buddhas.

It is wisdom to let what we take in
And what we retain

---

[2] Thig le

Be free in their own places.

When this comes down
The darkness is split by lightening.
Its descent makes everything happen.
There is a path for everyone.
The one who brings it down
Is the ancestor of all the Buddhas.

Its measure is a flickering of self-liberation.
Its eternity is the abode of light that appears before us.
Its degree of heat is that what we take on
And what we retain
Are pure in their own place.
Its result will be that those who have no Dharma
Are liberated in their own places,
Surrounded by entourages of the five embodiments of Buddhahood.

This is not a proclamation.
It is a great vision.
The great vision is a self-illuminating mandala.
Its source is the core of our awareness of wisdom.

Non-dual wisdom is a core that cannot be apprehended.
There is no real thing that is a circle,
Even though it may be the core of material entities.

Pristine non-duality:
This is the core of ignorance.
Being one-pointed without changing:
This is the core of changing.
The circumference of a circle:
This is the core of a wheel.
The appearance of wisdom by itself:
This is the core of our origin.
Being pristinely without birth:
This is the core of our ideas.
The lack of seeking that occurs by itself:
This is the core of our intellect.
Spontaneously-realized wisdom:
This is the core of our foundation.
Our result is our own level:
This is the core of delusion.

The Gods and the Demons Are Not Two

When we do not understand the instructions on the cores
They are like the jewels on Nanda's crown.[3]
When we do not understand the time for publishing
We are like the blind who lead the blind.
When we do not understand the measures and designations
We are like people who sell gold in lumps.
When we do not understand the measure of our times of delusion
We are like people who dance at a fork in the road.
When we do not understand the way it is with our foundation
We are like people who seek water in dry ravines.
When we do not know the boundaries of our path
We are like people who are lost without a trace on the empty plains.
When we do not understand that our results are in their own place
We are like people whose box of gold has fallen into the ocean.

Those who do not understand what this means
Are now the majority.
The seeds of freedom
Have been lost throughout the abodes of samsara.
The sprouts of enlightenment
Are being cut off at the roots.

Reality is moist,
But a great drought blazes.
Pristine non-duality has been lost
From the unborn harvest of the Dharmakāya
Into the objects of our intellects.

We have listened too much,
And have got lost on language, logic, and words.
Our unborn wisdom has been lost to our passiveness.
Those who continue to use mental prayers
As the objects of their intellect
Are a great faction.

There is no time to wake up.
The Dharmakāya is at our door.
If we listen to the experts

---

[3] Nanda is the king of the Nagas. It is said that the jewels on his crown are the most beautiful in the world, but they are beyond the reach of humans, due to their location.

As they tell their stories about the unborn
We will be stupefied.

There is no understanding that may be achieved by a search.
We cut through our desires,
And our hope for life.
We orient ourselves through time and through karma,
And we wander where we please.

If we did not carry the unborn
Within our ideas,
It would not be possible for us to recognize non-dual wisdom.

If we do not have a core:
That what we take in and what we retain
Are liberated in their own places,
Then we are like people who tie knots in the sky:
Nothing happens.

The wisdom that is synchronous is unborn.
If we did not carry a synchronous ignorance,
It would not be possible for a synchronously-born wisdom to occur.
Pristine wisdom is not something to search for or practice.

If we did not carry a search
As a burden for our intellects,
It would not be possible that there would be a time
When being self-liberated without a search might occur.
Pristine wisdom has no borders.
If a multitude of various signs were not evident
It would not be possible for wisdom without borders to occur.

The Dharmakāya is unborn.
It pervades everything.
If those who hold the Dharma
Were not carried along in samsara itself,
Their equanimity would be lost
On the objects of their intellects.

Some who listen are confused.
They do not understand that the three worlds are self-liberating,
So they lose the three bodies[4] to their intellects,

The Gods and the Demons Are Not Two

And to the prayers in their minds.

It is difficult to leave the intellect behind.
Those who do not understand what this means
Are the majority.

This is what the All Good One said:

I use blessings to instruct my entourage
In the pervasive self-luminescence of the five perfect Sambhogakāyas.
It is by my blessings that they are truly Buddhas,
And through my blessings their embodiment as pleasure occurs.

The blessings of self-illumination
Manifest as a Sambhogakāya,
And through its blessings there are five embodiments.

The Buddha is made up of a soul[5] that has five bodies.
The blessings of equanimity come to us through all of them.
A tongue trained in compassion will dawn on us,
As if it was our eyes.

Nirmaṇakāyas appear by themselves.
They are equally present everywhere,
Like the sun that rises in the sky.

The signs there are for those in the darkness
Are pure in their own place.

One body encompasses all things,
So it is a magnificent body.
This pervasive lord has five wisdoms.
They are there within us all,
As our own portion.
This is a magnificent self-luminescence.
Its blessings do not grow or shrink.
The self-luminescence of wisdom

---

[4] This refers to the three embodiments of the Buddha: the embodiments of the Dharma, of perfect pleasure, and manifest embodiments. In this translation these are presented with their Sanskrit names: Dharmakāya, Sambhogakāya, and Nirmaṇakāya.
[5] bDag nyid, Ātman

Is equally there within us all.

This is how I have described our being blessed by the truly perfected Buddha.

From the Tantra on the Non-duality of Gods and Demons, this is chapter one: The All Good One is Beyond the Dharma.

A DISCOURSE IN WHICH VAJRA DHARMA MATI BLESSES THE FIVE NIRMAṆAKĀYAS

Then again an embodiment of perfect pleasure and its manifestations, Vajra Dharma Mati, addressed the All Good One:

O Blessed One,
Glorious All Good One,
What is it like to be beyond the Dharma?
We are essentially for the Dharma.
Please speak on your liberation from it.

The teachers of the anti-Dharma
Were on the rise in Vaishali,
When an entourage of five Buddhas
Arrived in a single company with their manifestation:
The teacher Scattered Light Rays,[6]
At a very blissful location.

After they had arrived he blessed them,
Then he gave these instructions to our teacher Vajra Dharma Mati

Listen well!
Do not dismay!
The road is frightening.
Do not be terrified.

---

[6] 'Od zer 'gyed pa

I will explain that you must not be terrified
Just once,
Or for just a while,
Or for one second.

After he said this, he gave instructions:

For those who are endowed with the Sugata's
Embodiment of perfect pleasure,
And his five wisdoms,
The embodiment of wisdom
Is a brilliant illumination.

Nirmaṇakāyas,
Be they Vajra Dharma Mati or anyone else,
Are embodiments of wisdom that have a purpose.
The eye of the omniscient one is mighty.
Its form and its wisdom are one,
But they appear to have many differences.
Why do we so wander?

The five perfect Sambhogakāyas
Pervade as one,
So they are in a state of unity,
And do not fall to any sides.
They are liberated in their own place.

This is a wisdom of unlimited extent.
It manifests in five wondrous qualities by itself,
And appears as the five great ones.

For those who do not understand this,
The five embodiments,
While they have no position,
Are forced into partisan positions that lack understanding,
And as a result of these deviant positions and understandings
They do not reach any end.
They make their fruits be gone,
By themselves.

Their Dharma is only temporary.
It is extremely difficult for them to find any results
That will take them to the end.

The Gods and the Demons Are Not Two

Due to this difficulty,
I will teach on recognition.

The fathers and the mothers
Of the five families of Victorious ones
Are described as being male and female Vairochanas.
These are the teachings on their thrones:

Fearless self-liberation is a lion throne.
To use our power to work to help living things is an elephant.
To use our energy to be liberated into our own place
Is the best of horses.
To liberate the five poisons into their own place is a peacock.
To have completed the good work of a great quest is a soaring garuda.
To maintain good works that are not preferential is a precious jewel.
The five powers of wisdom are precious jewels.
To use methods to get out the Dharma is a moon throne.

The unchanging Vairochana
Has a body white in color.
He is unborn and unshaking,
So he is Vajrasattva.
There is a great effulgence to his blessings,
So he is an embodiment of Ratnasambhava.
He has no fault or filth,
So he is Amitabha.
His good works are self-originating,
So he is Amoghasiddhi.

This is the wheel by which the six classes of living beings
Are liberated into their own place,
And what it signifies:

The vajra is the unchanging
The precious jewel is the source of all good things,
The lotus is what sweeps filth away into its own place,
The cross is the sign by which samsara is sealed.

Their meanings and their signs
Are the perfection of the five powers.[7]

---

[7] dBang lnga

So it is that in cooperation with the five families,
We assign power at the center,
And make its aim our own.

We do not need to perform a summoning from Akaniṣṭa,
Or anything that would come from it.
We do not need to perform such things as
The generation of an enlightened attitude,
Or the performing of a summons.

O Noble-minded Vajra Dharma Mati,
Listen!

Our foundation is spontaneously formed.
Its horizons do not end.
Its wonder is its effulgent appearance in one place,
But when it is taken to represent a position,
The grounds for deviance there are in this
Are enormously great.

The sun is obstructed by the clouds,
So this cannot mean that it has clarity.
The embodiment of pleasure has been lost in appearances,
And cannot arise to liberate itself.
When there is nothing beyond the intellect,
Our path is one of delusion.
I am not proclaiming this to people of small intellect,
Whose attitude is one of prayer.

If we do not have a core
In which our positions and preferences
Are liberated into their own place,
The results of the designated meditations we do
Will not reach any conclusion.
We will be like parrots that expound on the Dharma:
We will drink our water with husks.

Explanations that use the mouth
Will not liberate us from taking a position.

If we do not understand that colors and jewelry
Illuminate wondrous things,
We will not become Buddhas

The Gods and the Demons Are Not Two

Through our meditations on jewels and costumes.

We may train monkeys to meditate,
But they will not know what it means.

We may caress our mouths with our ideas,
But we will not cut through to the root.

If we do not have a core,
A single letter of the roots of this heart-essence,
There will not come a time
When we approach the five families of Victorious Ones.

Optical illusions are like the things that drive us onward:
They are very far away.
How could it be that the problems and pleasures of the gods
Are non-dual?
If we had no core,
A synchronously-born god,
There would be no heart-essence for us to attain
Through our offerings to the five families of Victorious Ones.
The blessings of reality would only be partial,
So how would we get the supreme siddhi?

If we do not have a core
In which great compassion is apparent to us,
The compassion in the requests we make,
And in our going for refuge,
Would not reach any end.

We depend on just a single ray
From the luster of a thousand suns,
Glowing with dazzling compassion.
Our intellects happen to be small.

When we do not understand
That the five poisons are the best horses for the five bodies,
We may say that through meditation on these five bodies
The five poisons are pacified,
But when stupidity is the Dharmakāya,
The trunk of Vairochana is rotten.

There is a need for roots to make the leaves grow,
So it is that by pacifying the five poisons
We destroy the seeds for the five bodies.

Fruits do not come forth if there are no seeds.
Just so,
How will we achieve the five bodies
Without the five poisons?
Our objective is determined
By the real appearance of the five poisons.

The five bodies are self-apparent.
They are our senses.
We believe that without the five poisons
There would be no five bodies.

The five poisons have been publicized.
It is therefore necessary that they manifest as the five bodies.

When we understand the seeds of freedom
They are wondrous,
For we do not need to work on anything.

We do not look at the five poisons as problems.
It is clear that these five occur all by themselves.

These are the instructions on what they are in purity:

It is not necessary that the five poisons transform in station.
There is a continuity of self-originating presence.
When the poisons have no object
The result is that the core of their roots is cut.

To be entirely perfected without mixing things up
Is a true validation.
Our vow is not to fall into a bias,
Or to limit a vastness.
The thing we work to realize
Is that everything is perfected in the one.

A fitting analogy is that reflections appear on gold.

So he spoke.

From the Tantra on the Non-duality of Gods and Demons, this is chapter two: A Discourse in which Vajra Dharma Mati Blesses the Five Nirmaṇakāyas.

AN EXPLANATION OF THE BLESSINGS
OF THE THREE BODIES
OF THE CHILDREN OF THE VICTORIOUS ONES

Then Vajra Dharma Mati,
In a proper contemplation,
Asked:

Blessed All Good One,
Please explain the Nirmaṇakāyas
That are the children of the Victorious Ones.

Again the Blessed One gave instruction:

Listen,
Vajra Dharma Mati,
You!
I will teach you!

If we talk about the names for the Sambhogakāyas
Of the children of the Victorious Ones,
It is true that we may count the droplets in the ocean,
And that we may measure such things as rainbows in the mountains,
But who will be able to speak on the names there are for these?

In a single minute atom
There are Victorious Ones beyond counting.
When they coalesce,

The five Victorious Ones are apparent
In a single minute atom.

The material form of a minute atom
Is a child of the Victorious Ones, Vairochana.
His color is clear.
It is the child of the Victorious Ones, Vajrasattva.
Its true nature is his luminous appearance.
It is the Buddha Ratnasambhava.
It appears to have form, shape, and color.
It is the child of the Victorious Ones, Amitabha.
All of them in their entirety
Are realized without any bias.
In this they are Amoghasiddhi.
These are the Sambhogakāyas
Of the children of the Victorious Ones.

The five elements are the Nirmaṇakāyas
Of the children of the Victorious Ones.
They are inseparably in a state of a pure collective fulfillment.
For the children of the Victorious Ones,
This is the Dharmakāya.

There is not even one being
Who has not been empowered into this.
There is not even one being
Who has not received the empowerment.
There are no intervening spaces to this,
So all the empowerments are complete in a single instant.

Vajra Dharma Mati,
You!

You are empowered into the three bodies
Of the children of the Victorious Ones!
Do not hesitate for even an instant!
Do not postpone this for even an instant!

If it were possible to hesitate or postpone this,
That would put the children of the Victorious Ones a jump back,
And cause the Buddhas to jump ahead.
Our seeds of freedom would be lost for an eon!
We would not see the face of the Buddha,

But would wander around hopelessly.

The children of the Victorious Ones are manifestly embodied,
But we do not recognize them.
What appears to us is the Sambhogakāya,
But we do not believe it.
Anything that appears to us
Is a dawning of the Dharmakāya,
But we make no decisions.
All things are formed from themselves,
But we find no resolve.

E Ma Ho!
These are the instructions for the recognition
Of the five bodies in the apparent world:

Everything there is
Appears in five bodies.
This is definite.

Blessings shine out through the ten directions.
This is our belief.

All things arise within themselves.
This is definite.

When we recognize our own face by ourselves
We find resolve.

This is a knowledge of certitude.
It is realized within a single minute atom.
It is a wondrous thing.
It is manifest in every minute atom.
It is pervasive.
It is to be realized in each and every thing.
It is connected.

Everyone is in fact a child.
This is what we have to work on.

It is not possible that there be five bodies
That had no form.
This is a validation of their having a form.

Vairochana has arisen in a body of form.
This is his holy vow.

We say Vairochana is born,
But who does he appear to?
The fundament of life appears in a physical form.
If there was no form,
How could Vairochana have been formed?

The four waters of life are Vairochana.
If we reject them,
The roots of Vairochana will rot.
When we reject the four waters,
We throw away the seed of our embodiment.

These four: Birth, sickness, old age, and death
Are the four inner waters.
Who has seen Vairochana die?
If we understand that these four waters
Are Nirmaṇakāyas of the children of the Victorious Ones,
Then when we remove a manifest embodiment
Of a child of the Victorious Ones,
We battle at the door of birth.
We sever the transmission of the lineage
Of the embodiments of manifest compassion.

He who is the teacher of samsara
That severs the lineages of the Nirmaṇakāyas
Will have no support structure,
No miraculous birth,
No womb birth,
Nor any other.
He will not get the meaning of Nirmaṇakāya.
What a waste!
Will he continue to live like this?
Or will he wander?

If the Nirmaṇakāya is permanent
Our holy vow to manifest will be broken.
Anything we may manifest
Will be there for us.
This is what we have to work on.
This also validates the appearance of the six sages

As being unpredictable.

So he spoke.

Our minds are, themselves, unborn.
For the children of the Victorious Ones
This is the Dharmakāya.

The Dharmakāya is self-evident,
And is indivisible.
Its forms appear to us as many things.
We are liberated into a place where we do not give them up.

The Dharmakāya
Has been outlined to be a vessel and its contents,
But when we outline it in this way
We draw the Dharmakāya within us,
Even though its vastness is not an object for our awareness.

Our ideas about a degree of warmth will purify themselves.
Signs will be our objectives.
Our results will not be understandings, but equanimities.

Senses that have objects are self-liberating.
There are three mighty persons[8] who are generally pervasive.

So he spoke.

If we do not awaken
A contemplation of what is not the Dharma,
It will not be possible for our awareness
To be evident without an object.

If instantaneous self liberation does not occur,
The occurrence of a clear awakening
That has temporal reference
Will not be possible.
If the self-liberation of awareness does not happen,
It will not be possible for there to be a realm that has no location.

---

[8] dBang po mi gsum

If visible light had not been put into a system,
The occurrence of contemplations for which we desire signs
Would not be possible.
If we did not know the measure of the heat in our awareness,
We would not stop measuring our contemplations of the Buddha.

If we do not know our results to be
Our own share of what is not the Dharma,
We will be blocked by the time,
And it will be impossible to get them.

If we do not apply our senses to what we are capable of,
It will be impossible for our attitude of wishful thinking
To liberate us.
If we do not understand that this general pervasion
Is in our senses,
The achievement of the self-liberation of the six classes of living beings
Will not be possible.

To be finished with measuring is extremely dear.
We might be simply systematizing our logic,
But if we systematize it in a material form,
There will not be a time for the immaterial to occur.
If we do not go the measure of the immaterial,
There will not be a time for self-liberation to occur.
If we do not go the measure of self-liberation,
It will be impossible for a fully pure contemplation to occur.

If we do not go the measure of appearances,
It will be impossible for there to be a time
When the clear light will dawn.
If we do not go the measure of clear light
There will not occur a fully pure self-luminescence.
If we do not go the measure of our fundamental ground,
It will be impossible for there to be a time
When our results occur.
If we do not go the measure of our results,
Our transcending of the base will not occur.
If we do not make a system for the multitude of things,
There will not be a time in which we are omniscient.
If we do not publicize omniscience,
It will be impossible for the many to be self-liberated.

If we do not go the measure of the six classes of living beings,
There will not be a time in which the apparent world is entirely pure.

How will we change things,
So that the crevasses that hold the six classes of sentient beings
Are closed?
If we do not go the measure of delusion
There will not be a time in which self-liberation will occur.
If we do not go the measure of self-liberation
How will we ever be without delusion?

If we do not go the measure of the root of delusion
There will not be a time in which we turn away
From the results of our delusions.
If we do not go the measure of the results of our delusions
There will not be a time in which we cut their roots.

To be finished with the connections between all these things,
Their pervasiveness and their spontaneous realization,
Is dear.
To preach the Dharma without being finished with measures
Resembles blind people leading blind people.

If we do not understand that it is time for our results,
We are like the baby birds that come from rotten eggs.
If we do not understand the measure of the time for our practice,
We are one whose heart is a cavern or is made of earth.

If we do not understand the instructions on the core,
We are like eyes that do not move, but are forced downward.
If we do not understand the instructions on suppressing what is wrong,
We are like the partridges who land on top of tigers.

If we do not understand the instructions on measures,
This resembles an overflow when there is too much camphor.
If we do not understand the instructions on signs,
We are like the blind who hide boxes of gold.

If we do not understand the instructions on the measure of our heat,
We are like those with mantras who experiment with poisons.
If we do not go the measure of our blessings,
We are like those who rub mercury into rocks.

If we do not go the measure of the heart transmission,
We are like those who use their hands and feet in black darkness.
If we do not go the measure of the oral transmission,[9]
We are like people whose noses have been cut off,
Looking into a mirror.

If we do not go the measure of a vision of death,
We are like those who dream of a *bhihatsi*.
If we do not keep the measure of the three who remember.[10]
We are like people with mutilated hands who climb on the rocks.

If we do not go the measure of spontaneous realization,
We are like those who cover over their only jewel.
If we do not go the measure of a vast dimension,
There will not be a time in which our philosophical theories
Take their own place.

If we do not go the measure of having no position,
There will not be a time in which these vast dimensions are liberated.
If we do not make a system out of dualistic appearances
There will not be a time in which indivisibility will occur.

If we do not go the measure of indivisibility,
There will not be a time in which dualistic appearances
Are self-liberating.

So he spoke.

From the Tantra on the Non-duality of Gods and Demons, this is chapter three: An Explanation of the Blessings of the Three Bodies of the Children of the Victorious Ones.

---

[9] bKa' rgyud
[10] Dran po gsum po

SELF-LIBERATION
THROUGH RECOGNITION OF THE VIEW

Then again the most pure one exclaimed:

Listen,
Vajra Dharma Mati,
You!

I will teach you about Mara's field of practice.

What we call Mara
Is ignorance.
The foundation of Mara
Is stupidity.
Its cause is a synchronously-born ignorance.
The result is that the four Maras move through everything.
Our views are degraded into Maras.

Our views appear to be objects of emptiness.
Experts in wishful thinking,
Who use objects for their views,
Do not understand that we have a core
That is able to deal with conditions of sorrow.

We have been carried off by the thief-children
Of the Mara of our intellects.
Our views have been lost to thieves.

So how will we cut them off at the root?
Those who are the experts at cutting through
Are the thieves.
This is why those who lust after a thousand views
Are being stolen away by the Mara of desire.

Their views have been transformed
By conditions of sorrow.
They are being stolen away by the Mara of hatred.

They do not understand the methods
By which things are mixed into non-duality,
So they are being stolen away by the Mara of stupidity.

They consider their intellectual views to be good,
So they are stolen away by the Mara of pride.

They are habituated to the philosophical theories
That represent the views of their own scriptures,
So they are stolen away by the Mara of jealousy.

They do not understand
That the ability to handle conditions is self-liberating,
So they are tricked by the Mara of rage.

These six thieves have cut us off at the trunk.
The perspective in which things awaken themselves
Has been stolen by thieves.
If we do not cut these robbers off at the root,
There will not be a time in which we find the view.

If we are not freed from the Mara of desire,
We will be born along the avenues that bring results.

If we are not freed from the Mara of hatred,
We will surely be born in hell.

If we are not freed from the Mara of stupidity,
We will be born into the world of the animals.

If we are not freed from the Mara of pride,
We will be born into the world of humans.

The Gods and the Demons Are Not Two

If we are not freed from the Mara of jealousy,
We will surely be born in the world of the asuras.

If we are not freed from the Mara of rage,
We will also be born into the world of the asuras.

Moreover,
A single cause functions as six conditions.
The cause is primary.
Things are changed by conditions.

If our awareness does not arise within emptiness
There will not be a time in which these six conditions are self-liberating.
If these six conditions are not liberated into their own place
There will not be a time in which the six Maras are defeated.

If we do not recognize a person who has robbed us,
How will we ever recognize Mara?
If we do not recognize Mara,
How will we ever find the view?

The view does not fall to any side.
It has been blessed by Mara,
Then carried off onto his side.
If we do not understand that Mara has no position,
We will not get to a view that has no position.
We must cut off Mara's life-force at the root!

Wisdom exists without requiring a life–force,
So it cuts off the lives of the Maras within our views
At the root.

Self-liberation is pristine.
It is like a bird soaring through the sky of wisdom,
But it has been carried away by the Maras that are the vehicles.

Cravings and lusts are the Maras of appearance.
Distracting gatherings are what carry us away.
The Maras of distraction are pride, arrogance, and fame.
Distracting entertainments are what carry us away.

To cease speaking of our experiences
Is the Mara of a small intellect.

A Tantra of the Great Perfection

We are carried away by our addiction to receiving orders.

To listen much but proclaim meaningless things
Is the Mara of language.
We are carried away by the Maras of dissatisfaction.

Colors that appear by themselves
Are Maras of light.
We are carried away by the Maras of attachment and lust.

When we understand the core of the three kinds of wisdom[11]
We will be freed from the obstructions
Made by the Maras that are the vehicles.

When we understand the core of self-apparent lusts and cravings
Our gatherings will be liberated into their own place.

When we understand that the core of pride is equanimity,
We will be liberated into a self-apparent non-duality.

Our lusts and cravings will be set free on a path.
This will bring us experiences that are beyond the intellect.
We will be self-liberated from receiving orders.

The core that liberates our reputation and enjoyments
Into their own place
Also liberates our exaggerations into their own place.

When we understand the core of the self-appearing bardo
We will be liberated onto the path of lust and craving.

If we do not understand Mara's boundaries,
There will not be a time in which we are victorious over Mara.
If we do not know how to recognize Mara
There will not be a time in which we cut through our exaggerations.
If we do not understand that our exaggerations are self-liberating
There will not be a time in which the degree of our warmth
Will be self-liberating.

When we recognize Mara
We go for the eyes,

---

[11] Shes rab rnam gsum

The Gods and the Demons Are Not Two

Right away,
And not for the head or body.
His one eye and his thousand eyes
Look in the ten directions.

The king of the Maras has one eye.
The minister of the Maras has a hundred eyes.
He has no head or body,
But is proud of his eyes.

If we do not know how to recognize the eyes
Then where will we find words for the recognition of the Buddha?
There will not be a time
In which the Buddha manifests his self-liberation.

When we lack the core
Of an eye that sees without prejudice,
There will not be a time in which the great eye of wisdom dawns on us.
If we lack the core of a single eye that looks in the ten directions,
There will not be a time in which the one eye of wisdom dawns on us.

If we lack the core
To move through the sky with crippled feet,
There will not be a time in which we arrive anywhere,
For Buddhahood has no location.

If we do not understand the instructions
On taking lives with crippled hands,
There will not be a time in which we cut the roots
Of the life-force of samsara.

If we lack the core
Of a heart-desire for something that is immaterial
There will not be a time in which
Our guru's instructions will be made manifest.

If we lack a core that is disembodied,
And has no head or body,
There will not be a time in which
We divide our minds from our wisdom.

If we lack a core
That turns the wheels of the insubstantial,

There will not be a time in which
The clear light of wisdom dawns on us.

If we lack the core
To make determinations with rocks when there is no earth,
There will not be a time in which
The All Good One will arrive at his own place.

If we lack a core in which
We are liberated into our own place without bias,
There will not be a time in which we defeat
The armies of the Maras that make up our views.

So he spoke.

From the Tantra on the Non-duality of Gods and Demons, this is chapter four: Self-Liberation through Recognition of the View.

RECOGNIZING THE MEDITATOR
AND
CUTTING THROUGH THE ROOTS
OF LIFE AS A MARA

Then again he gave instructions:

Listen,
Vajra Dharma Mati,
You!

Mara is an obstruction for everyone.
Through being meditators,
We degrade ourselves into being Maras.

Mara's cause is grasping.
Mara's conditions are the objects we take in.
His result is the world, the abode of samsara.
If we are not free within the abode of samsara,
We have fallen under the control of Mara.

The blessings of Mara
Are our experiences of lust and craving.
Those who meditate on these things
Are degraded into Maras.
They have meditations with signs,
And meditations without signs.

Bliss and craving are Maras of lust.
Dark depression and jealousy are Maras of hatred.
Not knowing our own liberation is the Mara of stupidity.
Illuminating our own character is the Mara of pride.
Emptiness and the forms that it takes is the Mara of jealousy.
Not knowing how to blend things is the Mara of rage.

The root of Mara
Is ignorance.
Self-originating ignorance degrades us into Maras.

If he does not sever the root of Mara's life
A meditator will be blessed by Mara.
The experience is pleasant.
It gives us happiness,
But we will have fallen under the power of Mara.

It is just when our understandings are changed by conditions
That our understandings have been stolen by Mara.
When we think that our experiences are dependent on Mara
The things that we know have been blessed by Mara.
When we think about demonstrating our experience
We are brought under Mara's control.
When we think that there is something more clear than this,
We are blessed by Mara.

It is extremely difficult to finish with
The measure of Mara.
Everyone has been blessed by Mara,
So when we cut the root of Mara's life,
We must leap over the narrow passage[12]
Of our hopes and fears.

We may kill to the depths of the ocean.
We may kill to the peak of Mt. Meru.
We may kill right up to the sun and the moon.
We may kill to the peaks of white snow.
We may kill on the way to the mountains of stone.
We may kill up to the base of the mountains of stone.
We may kill to the summit of the three existences,
But if we do not have the core of the bottom of the ocean

---

[12] 'Phrang rgal. This word may be related to Thod rgal.

The Gods and the Demons Are Not Two

There will not be a time in which our habitual patterns are exhausted.
If we do not have the core of the peak of Mt. Meru,
There will not be a time in which self-liberation will dawn on us.
If we do not have the core of both the sun and the moon,
There will not be a time in which non-duality dawns on us.
If we do not have the core of the peaks of white snow,
There will not be a time in which we clean away our filth,
If we do not have the core of the way to the mountains of stone,
There will not be a time in which the pristine will dawn on us.
If we do not have the core of the base of the mountains of stone,
There will not be a time in which we are liberated from failure.
If we do not have the core of the summit of the three existences,
There will not be a time in which our three embodiments
Will be self-liberated.

The mind, wisdom, and habitual tendencies are three.
The base, the path, and the fruit are three.
The basis for delusion, the delusion, and the entity are three.
The methods for revolt, the borders, and the results are three.
A blessing, a wave, and a structure are three.
Awakening, being awoken, and freshness are three.
Primordial, knowledge, and wisdom are three.
The Dharma, the embodiment, and non-conceptuality are three.
The Dharma, the one who has a Dharma, and reality are three.
Karma, emanation, and the lengthening of time are three.
Tendencies, attachments, and changes are three.
Self, originating, and wisdom are three.

These triads are not ornamented by any instructions.
They are presented here merely as general combinations.
If we do not understand that our target is white at the back,
And we do not understand the suppression of what is wrong,
Our reality will be stolen away
Into the common ground

The difference between being general and being particular
Is dear.
The core,
The suppression of what is wrong
And the removal of obstacles
Are three.

Our meditation must use the specifics there are
On the contemplations of the deceitful
So that we may recognize demons and thieves.

It is just when we get carried away
By the demon[13] of meditation
That we are blessed by the Mara of pride.
If we do not cut through the root of this Mara
There will be no time in which the filth of our delusions
Will be cleansed.
If we do not cut through the root of the life of this demon
There will be no time in which we cut through
The roots of the three realms.

Demons are the seeds of freedom.
It is because they are free
That they may be neither liberated nor depleted.
These are the instructions of a properly perfected one.

When we desire freedom
We give birth to ideas.
Ideas are the seeds of freedom.
Who is there that thinks about being non-conceptual?

If we desire enlightenment
We are obstructed.
Through our meditation on peaceful abiding
The roots of a higher vision are rotted.
Through meditations that cling to a mind
The roots of self-liberation are rotted.
Through meditating on happiness
The roots of non-duality are rotted.
Through meditations that have signs
The roots of pristine awareness are rotted.
Through meditating on the mouths of others
The roots of a mute mouth are rotted.
Through meditating on a mute mouth
The roots of other people's mouths are rotted.
Through meditation on non-duality
The roots of interactivity are rotted.

---

[13] 'Dre

The Dharmas that a meditator creates
And their impermanence
Are assumed to be a duality,
But by making this assumption,
We are not given any liberation into our own place.

Those who continue with this
May be deluded about their objectives,
But a recognition of wisdom will come to them by itself
In their own ideas.
On the great road of freedom
They will plant the trunk of enlightenment.
Their intellects will be equanimous and without ideas.
They will be totally liberated.

When we have no desire for enlightenment
We will realize the Dharmakāya spontaneously.

We will be finished with saying:
"Peaceful abiding is self-liberating,"
And wisdom will dawn on us.

We will awaken in splendor from our clingings,
Expanding into the self-originating Dharmakāya.

Without our meditating on great bliss,
The Dharmakāya dawns from within us.
Without our meditating on any signs,
Our self-appearance shines through the five bodies.

Without meditating on the mouths of others
Our self-appearance manifests without being objectified.
Without meditating on being mute,
Our lack of any object manifests as our self-liberation.

Without a meditation on non-duality,
Our self-appearance is spread out in a circle.[14]
The actor is beyond effulgence and awakening,
Without acting as a meditator.

---

[14] Thig le

The Dharmakāya is a self-originating non-duality.
This occurs to us by itself.
When we understand that this is how it is,
We attain freedom as a result.

An attainment that does not fall to any extreme
And a liberation into our own place
Are dear.

So he spoke.

From the Tantra on the Non-duality of Gods and Demons, this is chapter five: Recognizing the Meditator and Cutting through the Roots of Life As A Mara.

THE RECOGNITION OF MARAS
IN OUR PRACTICE

Then again he gave instructions:

Listen,
Vajra Dharma Mati,
You!

Everyone has been blessed by Mara.
Our practices have been degraded into Maras.

The thing we call a Mara is ignorance.
We do not recognize the doer of our practice.
Ignorance is our degradation into Maras.

The ten external Dharma practices,
And the wisdom we use for our views
And for our meditations and practices,
Are practices that relate to external objects.

The appearance of methods is the Mara of attachment.
We are tied up in the Root Tantra's noose,
And blessed by the Mara of lust.

The spirit of pride is to move through bliss,
But we have a lack of clarity in our nerves and channels.
This is the Mara of hatred.

A Tantra of the Great Perfection

The lack of understanding of self-liberation
Is the Mara of stupidity.

The wish to destroy others is the Mara of jealousy.
The purification of our nerves and channels is the Mara of rage.

You must understand that these are the facilitators[15] of the Maras.

If we do not have a core of awareness that has no object,
We will be jealous regarding the chakras of the nerves,
And we will be blessed by the Mara of fantasy.
It makes us think about eliminating the empty spaces in our nerves.
This is the blessing of Mara.

Our consciousness is forced inside of our nerves.
Mara has stolen our understanding.

We stamp our bliss with the seal of emptiness.
We have fallen under the control of Mara.

When we finally understand that appearances are empty
We will have learned the majesty
Of the empty spaces[16] in our nerves.

When our awareness is finally pristine,
Our consciousness will be thrust into the *awadhuti*.
When this finally happens there will be an inner clarity
That has no location.
This is an interaction between bliss and emptiness.

When the flashing finally manifests as being self-liberated
We have internalized clarity and emptiness.
If we do not have a core
In which we are empty of any true nature,
Our enumeration of the nerves at the navel will deviate.
This will obstruct our learning about the empty spaces.

If we do not have a core in which our compassion is unstoppable
We will deviate from the doors of the secret nerves.

---

[15] mKhan po
[16] sTong ra

This will obstruct our recognition of bliss.

If we do not have a core in which our qualities are unchanging
We will deviate in our practice
Of folding in the nerves at the heart.
This will obstruct our stamping them
With the seal of emptiness.

If we do not have a core in which our good works are unhindered,
Due to these obstructions,
We will deviate in our practice
Of counting the nerves at the crown of our heads.
This will obstruct us from stamping the seal of bliss and emptiness.

If we do not have the nerve to have unstoppable compassion,
And a manifest embodiment of compassion does not appear,
The sage will have no means
By which to lead the six classes of living beings.

If we do not have the nerves for a stupidity that does not open,
There will be no way to teach us about
The all-encompassing Dharmakāya.

If we do not have the nerve of a shining essence
There will be no way for our visions
To manifest as a Sambhogakāya.
If our own visions do not manifest as a Sambhogakāya
This will cut the flow
Of the wonders of the Dharmakāya.

If we cut the flow of the wonders of the Dharmakāya
There will be no way for the two form embodiments to manifest.

If we do not have the nerve for uninterrupted good works
The virtues of the three embodiments will be cut off at the ends.
The Dharmakāya is not an object for our senses.
If it were, this would negate a wisdom that is a knowledge.

If we do not have the nerve to have good qualities that do not change
The three embodiments will turn out to be
Both impermanent and compounded.

If the three embodiments are impermanent and compounded
There will be no need for a recognition of a result.

If we do not have the nerve of a closed stupidity,
Who will fabricate sensory organs for the Dharmakāya?
The seeds of the Dharmakāya
Will be rotted at the roots.

If stupidity does not manifest as self-liberating,
Who will fabricate a sure knowledge
Of the Dharmakāya?

If stupidity does not manifest as pristine awareness,
Where will we look for a Dharmakāya
That is able to handle conditions?

If stupidity does not manifest without an object,
What will we call the measure
Of the knowledge of the Dharmakāya?

If stupidity does not manifest as being pure by itself,
Who will we teach the results of the Dharmakāya?

If we do not have the nerve for compassionate desire,
Who will have the identity of a Nirmaṇakāya?
The seeds for a Nirmaṇakāya will have rotted.

If desire does not manifest as self-liberating,
Who will have a sure knowledge of the Nirmaṇakāya?
If desire does not manifest as pristine awareness
Who will there be that can handle the conditions
Of being a Nirmaṇakāya?
If desire does not manifest as being non-dual,
Who will take measure of a Nirmaṇakāya's knowledge?
If desire does not manifest as being pure in itself,
Who will we teach the majesty of a Nirmaṇakāya?

If we do not have the nerve for an essence that is luminous,
Who will fabricate sensory organs for the embodiment of pleasure?
The seeds for the embodiment of pleasure will have rotted.

If we do not understand that hatred is self-liberating,
How will we have any sure knowledge of the Sambhogakāya?

If hatred does not manifest as pristine awareness,
Who would hope to be able to handle the conditions
Of being an embodiment of pleasure?

If hatred does not manifest as an inner clarity,
What will we call the measure
Of the knowledge of the Sambhogakāya?
If hatred does not manifest as total purity,
What would the recognition of the Sambhogakāya be?

The two nerves possess wondrous aspects.
When we understand that hatred is self-liberating,
We will need the red instructions[17]
On the suppression of the wrong kinds of hatred.

When we understand the core
Of the red instructions on the suppression of what is wrong,
The Sambhogakāya will be manifest in our own vision.
This is not ordinary.
It is supreme.

When we understand that stupidity is self-liberating,
We will need the instructions on the intentional cycles[18]
For the suppression of what is wrong.
If we understand the core
Of the intentional cycles in the suppression of what is wrong,
The Dharmakāya will manifest for us,
Without being an object.

When we understand that desire is self-liberating,
The instructions on the core cycles of signs[19] are dear.
When we understand the meaning of the core,
And the cycles of the signs,
The Nirmaṇakāya will be made manifest
On its own behalf.

If we use these six things to understand the core,
A conviction that it not proud will dawn within us.

---

[17] dMar khrid
[18] Don skor
[19] brDa skor gnad

We will have cut off our pride,
At the root.
We will have grasped the supreme sign,
Which is to be desireless.
The three embodiments will have dawned within us,
And we will have a compassion that has no object.

Buddhahood has no object.
If our awareness does not manifest without an object,
It will be extremely difficult to have any Buddhahood,
For it has no object.

If pride does not manifest as self-liberating,
It will be difficult for a contemplation of the Buddha to dawn on us.

If a lusty disposition does not manifest as self-liberating,
It will be extremely difficult for the three embodiments
To liberate themselves.

It is because it is difficult
That it is easy.
It is because it is easy
That it is difficult.

The shortest of the short is long.
The longest of the long is short.
The greatest of the great is small.
The smallest of the small is great.
For these reasons,
It is most difficult to measure anything.

So he spoke.

From the Tantra on the Non-duality of the Gods and the Demons, this is chapter six: The Recognition of Maras in our Practice.

A PRESENTATION ON RESULTS

Then the most pure one gave an instruction:

Listen,
Vajra Dharma Mati,
You!
I will teach you about the fields of practice
And the blessings
Of Maras and of demons.[20]

When our results have been degraded into being Maras,
Our results will have purpose,
And be referred to according to the time.
We will have been blessed by the Mara of stupidity.

When our results have turned into objects for our desirous disposition,
We have been carried away by the Mara of desire.

When our results are in reference to time
They are far away
We have been carried away by the Mara of hatred.

When our results are the scriptures that characterize the vehicles.
We have been blessed by the Mara of jealousy.

---

[20] 'Dre

We make ourselves think that we ourselves will get our results.
We have been blessed by the Mara of pride.

When our results are not something we understand.
We have been blessed by the Mara of rage.

We have, then, two ultimate fruitions,
But they are similar, alike, and analogous,
So we are going to be mistaken!

The three embodiments that are specifically ordinary
And the three supreme embodiments that are pristine
Are two,
But they are similar, alike, and analogous,
So we are going to mistake them!

The cleansing of the nerves and channels of our awareness
And the cleansing of the nerves and channels of our methods
Are two,
But they are similar, alike, and analogous,
So we are going to mistake them!

The result of getting something that we desire into our dispositions
And the result of self-evident awareness
Are two,
But they are similar, alike, and analogous,
So we are going to mistake them!

The Buddhahood that is very famous and is generally pervasive
And the Buddhahood that has a self-evident significance
Are two,
But they are similar, alike, and analogous,
So we are going to mistake them!

We do not set a time for our results.
This is because nothing comes before or after wisdom.
We do not desire our results to be in the bardo,
For they are pristine in their non-duality.

We do not desire to reverse our delusions,
For we are at one with non-delusion.
We do not desire a result that is a clinging to our mind,
For we cling to pristine awareness.

The Gods and the Demons Are Not Two

We do not desire the experience of happiness,
For bliss dawns on us in pristine purity.

It is right when we illuminate the appearances of delusion
That we become mighty ones who have no delusions.
Our conviction is that delusions are unborn.

When things manifest as delusions,
That is the best of signs.
The pristine purity of our delusions
Is the measure of our warmth.

Self-evident delusions are a knowledge that is sure.
The recognition of Mara is a validation.
Delusion is an empowerment of wisdom.
It is a result that has no exterior or interior.

It is right when our self-appearance manifests in total purity,
That we are mighty ones who have obliterated
The Maras that are our emotional problems.

Our conviction is that this is self-evident and pristine.
Self-liberating appearance is the measure of our warmth.
The self-appearance of the unborn
Is the best of signs.
The recognition of this self-appearance
Is a knowledge that is sure.
The recognition of self-appearance is our validation.

Self-evident wisdom is the method to be used
For imparting empowerments.
It appears by itself without any object.
It is a method for the practice of empowerment.
The result of the empowerment is that we are
In possession of the five great ones.[21]

This self-appearance is neither outside nor inside us.
This is the conviction of the empowerment.
We bring whatever appears under our control.
This is our warmth,
And it is our validation.

---

[21] Che ba lnga.

Self-appearance manifests as many things.
This is the sign of the empowerment.
The knowledge of unity
Is the recognition of the empowerment.
The knowledge of these things
Is the empowerment that is evident to us.

It is right when we liberate the six communities into their own places,
That we become mighty ones
Who have obliterated the Maras of the children of the gods.
Our conviction gathers these six communities in a flash.
The flash is self-liberating.
This is our warmth and our validation.

When the flashes flicker in many ways
That is the best of signs.
To take this flashing in by its face:
That is recognition.

The flash has no breath.
It is a recognition.
It is unimpeded, pristine, and breathless.
It is the method by which we grant empowerment.

The understanding that the measure of the flickering
Is pure within its own place
Is the acquisition of the empowerment.

The practice of the empowerment
Brings the dawning of this pristine flashing.
We will find no object for this flashing.
This is the result of the empowerment.
The whiteness and blackness of this flashing
Are our convictions about the empowerment.
The three kinds of appearances
Are assembled flashings.
This is our warmth and our validation.

Without this flashing
There would be no Buddha.
This is the sign of the empowerment.
The flashing will be a flickering

That may be either subtle or coarse.
It is a recognition of our pristine awareness.
When we understand the suppression of what is wrong,
We will empower the six communities.

It is right when non-dual wisdom dawns on us,
That we become mighty ones
Who have obliterated the Maras of the five heaps.
Our conviction is that wisdom dawns on us self-evidently.
The birth of a variety of things to take in and hold onto
Is our warmth and our validation.

When subjects and objects manifest without being born
That is the best sign.
The recognition of subjects and objects that reaches to the core
Is wisdom.
The non-duality of subjects and objects
Is our method for granting empowerments.

Our retention of this
Is self-originating and self-evident.
It is the attainment of the empowerment.
The understanding that this retention is unborn
Is the practice of the empowerment.

The dawning of Buddhahood has no location.
It is the result of the empowerment.
Pristine non-dual wisdom
Is the conviction of the empowerment.
Non-duality is pure within its own place.
This is our warmth and our validation.

The birth of a variety of understandings about this retention
Is the sign of the empowerment.
The understanding that we are self-liberated,
Without our holding onto anything,
Is the recognition of the empowerment.
The understanding of these things
Is the unsurpassed fruition of the empowerment.

It is right when pristine stainlessness dawns on us,
That we become mighty ones who have obliterated
The Mara of the lord of the dead.

Our conviction is pristine delusion.
Unborn pristine awareness is our warmth and our validation.
Birth and death are the best signs.
Unborn unity[22] is the sure knowledge of the empowerment.
The four pristine waters are its recognition.

The self-liberation of birth and death
Is the method for imparting the empowerment.
To understand that birth and death are pure in themselves
Is the acquisition of the empowerment.
The dawning of unborn wisdom
Is the practice of the empowerment.
The liberation of the four waters into their own places
Is the result of the empowerment.
To cut the river of birth and death
Is the conviction of the empowerment.
To turn away from saying what is apparent and what is real
Is the warmth and the validation of the empowerment.

The conviction that all living beings are pervaded by the four waters
Is the sign of the empowerment.
The recognition of the empowerment
Makes these four waters manifest without pollution.
The four waters are self-liberating.
This is the granting of the empowerment into the unified circle.[23]

The vastness of self-liberated appearance is not limited.
It is what imparts the empowerment for the Tantra.
Totality is full within ourselves.
This is the way to receive the empowerment.
To have no position and to not be limited
Is the practice of the Tantra.
There is nothing inside of us.
This is the result of the Tantra.
All things are perfected into one.
This is the essence of the Tantra.
All things are connected and are pure.
These are the words of assurance.

---

[22] Nyag gcig
[23] Nyag gcig thig le

The Gods and the Demons Are Not Two

Our self-appearance is totally pure.
This is the proper granting of the empowerment.
Our awareness is stainless.
This is the proper acquisition of the empowerment.
To cease with the flashing and be stainless.
This is the proper practice.
When the flashing transforms into something that we ourselves control,
That is the result.

There is no great self-evident unobstructedness.
Compassion is equally present in everyone.
It is like sesame oil.

The nine gods take their part
As gods who flash through eight communities.
The three times are indivisible.
The unified circle is a *kapala*.

All things are formed by themselves,
And their formation is truly unified.
When our awareness is stainless,
We will have properly succeeded.

When the apparent world manifests as a unity,
There is the granting of the *Phurpa* empowerment.
When the four Maras are evident to us in a single recognition
That is the granting of the empowerment of ambrosia.
When our vision is degraded into being a Mara,
There remains an ambrosial conviction.

The five Maras are apparent to us,
And we understand their ambrosia,
So we are mighty ones.
When we have cut through the poisons at their roots
Buddhahood will manifest as ambrosia.
That is our warmth and our validation.

The five poisons manifest
As eighty-four thousand emotional problems.
They are the major signs for there being ambrosia.
The teaching that the five poisons are flashing ambrosias
Is a recognition of ambrosia.
To manifest every ambrosia,

None excepted,
Is the transmission of the vase of ambrosia.

When we are entirely finished with everything,
The empowerment of the transmission has been imparted.
Everyone is already in their own place,
So they have received the empowerment of the transmission.

The understanding that everything is self-originating
Is the practice of the transmission.
To be done with the play
Of holding hands with the Buddha
Is the fruit of this transmission.

There are three kinds of ambrosia that are meaningful:

Ambrosias made of material things that are combined into medicines
Are external ambrosias.
Those that work to transform the five poisons into five gods
Are internal ambrosias.
The recognition that the deterioration into being a Mara
Stops the flashing,
And is an ambrosia,
Is the secret ambrosia.

That which is called a Mara
Is ignorance.
The liquid[24] is the wisdom to be self-aware.
An essential ingredient in ambrosia
Is the absence of any flashing.
This is the greatest medicine,
Made from extracted nutrients.
The material substances may be of various kinds.
Its liquidity is the pristineness of wisdom.
Its natural form is also called: "Ambrosia."
We take it up into our hands constantly,
So it is also called: "The ambrosia that we work with."

---

[24] The word "ambrosia" in Tibetan is bDud rtsi, which literally means "Mara juice" or "liquid Mara." The word is broken in half and then commented on in this and the following verses.

It is because we will have recognized Maras
That they manifest as liquid.
This is called: "The true ambrosia."

The source from which ambrosia appears
Is the sky of the father.
The father is the All Good One.
The vessel that cradles the ambrosia
Is the All Good Mother.
Their blessings are the cause for the ambrosia's emergence.
The vessel that cradles the ambrosia
Is an abode in which its manifestations will appear.

Their flashing is the cause for the emergence of the ambrosia.
The vessel that cradles the ambrosia
Is this pristine flashing.
The cause for which the ambrosia emerges
Is to flash through the eight communities.[25]

The vessel that cradles the ambrosia
Is an abrupt penetration of the six communities.
The cause for which the ambrosia emerges
Is the rage of the five poisons.

The vessel that cradles the ambrosia
Is self-evident self-liberation.
The cause for which the ambrosia emerges
Is what we take in and what we hold onto.
The vessel that cradles the ambrosia
Is the great method of non-duality.

The cause for which the ambrosia emerges
Is ignorance and lack of understanding.
The methods for mixing the ambrosia
Are awareness and understanding.

The cause for which the ambrosia emerges
Is lust and hatred.
The method for mixing the ambrosia
Is to be without lust or its objects.

---

[25] Tshogs brgyad. This refers to the eight consciousnesses as described by the Yogacara school.

The cause for which the ambrosia emerges
Is the five poisons and the three poisons.
The measure to which the ambrosia is to be mixed
Is coordinated with our body, speech, and mind.

The mightiest ambrosia is made with the five poisons.
The virtue of this ambrosia
Is that it is made with the five wisdoms.
The sure knowledge of ambrosia
Is that it is a flash of self-liberation.
The temperature of the ambrosia
Is in the privacy of the flashing.

The symbols for the ambrosia
Are made by our eighty-thousand emotional problems.
The conviction of the ambrosia
Is that it is a recognition of our body, speech, and mind.

The fruition of the ambrosia
Is a pristine stainlessness.
The essence of the ambrosia
Is a wisdom that is knowledge.
The definition of ambrosia
Is that it is stainlessly pure.
The division of the ambrosia
Is that there are three primary sorts.

A fitting analogy for ambrosia
Is that it is unpolluted by misunderstandings.

It is right when everything comes to its core
That we explain what is called
The imparting of the empowerment of the upadeśa.

We find the totality of our resolve,
And take it to the core.
This is also called:
"Receiving the empowerment of the upadeśa instructions."

This is the imparting of the empowerment for the Ati:

A is the unborn.
Ti is the awareness, the embodiment of the vajra.
This is the imparting of the empowerment of the Ati
Into which the six communities are not born.

A is the self-liberation of the six communities.
Ti is the unchanging embodiment of these six communities.

A is that the flashing is not born.
Ti is the pristine, the embodiment of stability.

The essence of this upadeśa is significant.
Our foundation is of little toil and of great purpose.
Its definition is that everything is gathered at the core.
Its divisions are methods and wisdom.
A fitting analogy is that this resembles
A medicine that makes us miserable.

When we understand these things,
We will have been granted the empowerment of the upadeśa.

So he spoke.

From the Tantra of the Non-duality of the Gods and the Demons, this is chapter seven: A Presentation on Results.

A DESCRIPTION OF THE DHARMAKĀYA'S BLESSINGS UPON THE SAMBHOGAKĀYA

Then the most pure one exclaimed:

Listen,
Lord of Secrets,
You!

The self-evidence of the appearance of the five elements
Is the sky of A.
This and the three vajras will be used
To explain the imparting of the empowerment for vision.

When we understand the significance
Of the three kinds of sky,
We will not depend on the five elements.

When we understand the significance of the three kinds of vajra,
We will not rely on a body, speech, or mind.

When we understand the three cores of A,
We will not depend on the five wisdoms.

This is a description of the sky,
An opening of our understanding into the essence of the sky.
Its definition is that it is pervasive.

Its divisions are:
The sky that has color,
The sky that is an eternity of ornamented openings,
And the sky of true reality.
A fitting analogy is that this is like sesame and its oil.
A symbolic analogy is that
The sky is not more prominent than the five elements.

The sky of effulgent awareness
Is more important than our body, speech, and mind.
The sky in its proper meaning
Is the highest summit
In the construction of the three embodiments.

The sky of effulgent awareness
Is the five elements and the senses.
When awareness dawns on itself,
There is recognition.
It dawns without being either external or internal.
This is its warmth and its validation.

When we take the five elements on the path,
We are able to handle its conditions.
The teaching that the five elements are aware
Is recognition.
When the five elements manifest without there being any location,
That is the result.

So he spoke.

The sky in its proper significance
Is the power of the unified circle.
Pristine awareness is a knowledge of certitude.
Pristine appearance is its warmth and its validation.
Both objects and minds are liberated into their own place.
This is the knowledge of certitude.

When our own self-evidence dawns on us,
We will be able to handle the conditions.
When our self-evidence manifests as the clear light of wisdom,
That is recognition.
When our subjective reality manifests in a self-evident clear light,

The Gods and the Demons Are Not Two

That is the result.

So he spoke.

Again he gave instructions:

The essence of A is that subjective realities are unborn.
Its definition is that it is unchanging.
Its divisions are:
The A of our foundation, our path, and our result.

The A of our foundation
Is the topic to be discussed.
All things emerge from within the A.
She is the mother who gives birth to the three kinds of vision.

On the head of A
There are shoulders, hands,
And a body with five feet.

She is the grandmother
Who is the progenitor of us all.
She has moved from her place
To become the identity of the populace.

If we do not cut through to the roots of the populace
They will not come in contact with our philosophical theories,
But immediately upon cutting through to the roots of the populace
They will find a definitive certitude about our philosophical theories.

The six classes of living things
Are full within the body of the A.
They are perfected in the four secret seeds,
Which are called: A Nri Pre Du Su Tri.

A is the generator of all the letters.
It is not a substantial thing,
But is complete in what it means.
As an analogy,
It is like a colored rainbow that knows our path.
It is like blowing on a water crystal,
Or a fire crystal:
There is nothing substantial,

But at the foundation we succeed.

This is the tradition of the twelvefold dependent connections.
We continue to be in the tradition of samsara.

As an analogy,
It is like monkey fat on a smelting pot:
A cause is transformed into a condition,
Without doing anything special.
There is a transformation,
But the essence of the gold is one.
Those who are experts on gold will recognize this.

In the same way,
All Dharmas are one when we recognize them.
This is called: "The internalization of every Dharma."

As an analogy,
This resembles a turtle with a jewel stuck in its throat.
It can neither vomit it out forward,
Nor get it to move backward.
When we understand that all Dharmas lack locations,
There is no place where we wake up and grow into Buddhas,
Nor do we go to hell.

We neither come nor go.
Our five ways to transcend things
Are fulfilled within the A.

The Sambhogakāya is an Oṃ,
Which transforms into a trunk,
Perfecting the secret seeds:

Oṃ Ā: Hūṃ Svāhā

The vajra recitation is complete.

The unborn circle[26] is the seed[27] of a woman.
The place where we stop complicating the unborn
Is the seed of our taste.

---

[26] Thig le
[27] Sa bon

The Gods and the Demons Are Not Two

The five lights from the unborn clear light
Are the seeds of the months and days.
The pristine nature of Dharmas
Is the seed of the A.
The thing that shows us unborn unity
Is the seed of the A.

Everything is subsumed within our foundation.
This perfects the seed of the Hūṃ.
The mother that is our foundation
Does not change her own place.
This perfects the seed of the Svā.
She does not change and does not stop.
This perfects the seed of the Hā.

The O transforms into five bodies,
Holders of the five wisdoms.
The seeds of light for our body and our wisdom are complete.
The empty circle has five letters:

The A is dark blue,
The Hūṃ is white.
The Svā is yellow.
The Aṃ is red.
The Hā is green.
The seeds for the five secret lights
Are complete in our foundation.

A is the eye to which everything is perfect.
Its formation into five colors
Gives us an eye to which they are fundamentally perfect.
I bow to the eye that holds five lotuses.

The symbolic eye is the dawning of the five lights.
It is formed in the place for the Ha of our foundational mother.
A recognition of the view
Within the symbols for our embodiment and our wisdom
Is dear.

The symbols for the five lights,
And the significance they retain,
Is the eye of a lotus.
I bow to the eye of the open lotus.

You are the eye of the wisdom
Of a secret awareness.
Citta Rāja Guhya Prasara.
Your body and your wisdom shine.

O Eye of Wisdom,
I bow to the eye that is an open white lotus.
Guhya Mahā Prajñā Phala Eka Tila Prasara.

You are the eye of pristine wisdom.
You are the three embodiments that are our results,
That can neither be gained nor lost.
You are the eye of omniscience.
I bow to you.

Jñāna Cakṣu Sarva Eka Tila Guhya Tantra Upadeśa |
Mahā Cakṣu Prabeśaya |

You crack the shells of the eggs of ignorance,
And have an eye that makes a light of compassion.
You are the one stainless eye of wisdom.
I bow to you.

Abi Manu Prasara Cakṣu Bidha Jñāna Mahā

The Buddha retains a body of wisdom.
I bow to the eye that does not lust for wisdom.

The five kinds of transcendence
Are the five secret seeds.

The transcendence of Nri
Is a flashing over the grounds of our clarity.

The transcendence of A is a transformation into an Oṃ,
Which is the five naturally great things.[28]

The transcendence of Su is to pervade the nature of the A.

---

[28] Rang bzhin chen po lnga

The Gods and the Demons Are Not Two

The transcendence of Pre is the transformation of the Aṃ
Into a compassionate leader for those who live.

The transcendence of Du transforms into a god.
It is the eye that knows all secrets.

Through the understanding of this empowerment into the secret seeds
We eliminate our falling into the crevasses
That are the six classes of living things.

Manuśa Preta Katiraya Naraka Suryaka |
Dewa Akṣaloka |
Kora Kuru Svasti Mahā Prajñā Phala |
Eka Thila Bidya Jñāna Cakṣu.

So he spoke.

Now I will explain the meaning of vajra.

Vajrakāya Jñāna Ratna Phala Pariśuddha A.

The meaning of vajra has three aspects:

The vajra of method, which is exemplified,
The symbolic vajra that tames those who live,
And the vajra in its proper significance.

The vajra of method that is to be exemplified
Is cast out of gold and silver,
Or drawn in a painting.
What we call a vajra is a dorje.[29]

Kāya is the embodiment of the Dharma
Jñāna is great wisdom.
Ratna is a jewel.
Phala is good.
Pariśudha is stainless purity.
A exemplifies unborn reality.

Vajra Trikāya Pañca Buddhāya.
The three-pointed vajra exemplifies the three embodiments.

---

[29] rDo rje is the Tibetan word for vajra.

Its facing downward symbolizes the triad of body, speech, and mind.
There are five, to exemplify that each has the five wisdoms:
Each body has five wisdoms.

Pristine one-pointedness exemplifies the five kinds of transcendence.
The round part in the middle exemplifies the unified circle.
The wrathful face exemplifies the two kinds of form embodiments.
The vajra mandala is a symbol for self-originating methods.

The symbolic vajra demonstrates the perfection of our own bodies.
We join the bottoms of our feet
And the palms of our hands
To do the generation:

Vajra Kala Trijñāna Pañca Buddha'o

Our navel is the Dharmakāya,
And has no pain.
The stainless Dharmakāya pervades everything.

We push our hands upward,
Palms joined,
To symbolize the three embodiments.
We join the bottoms of our feet
To symbolize the three hearts.[30]

Our five fingers symbolize the five wisdoms.
Our face is a symbol for the appearance of our two form embodiments.
This is made manifest by itself,
So it is a vajra symbol.
The vajra, in its proper significance,
Is the wisdom in our awareness that perfects our three embodiments.

Vidya Jñāna Kasitrala Yogi |
Sarva Pañca Guhya Samaya Mudra Mahā Phala Ratna Tantra A Ka.

There are five poisons,
Five bodies,
And five wisdoms.

---

[30] Thugs gsum

The Gods and the Demons Are Not Two

The five poisons are our bodies, speech, and minds.
The five transcendences are a pristine circle of self-liberating awareness.
The flash of a wrathful face is the two form embodiments.
The four bodies at our navel liberate our pain into its own place.
A pristine flashing unifies the three embodiments at their summits.
If the five bodies were not the controllers
Of both the bodies and their five wisdoms,
We would not find any resolve or certitude
On what it means to be an embodiment or a wisdom.

If the winds of lust and hatred
Did not give birth to the five poisons,
To whom would there appear
A wisdom of some higher perception,
That is able to handle conditions?

If self-originating lust and hatred
Did not give birth to the five poisons,
Who would take measure of the heat
Of self-originating wisdom?

If we do not understand that the five poisons
Are our bodies and our wisdoms,
Who will be the mighty one
That recognizes the wisdom of self-awareness?

If the five poisons did not manifest
As eighty thousand emotional problems,
Who would it be that would recognize the wisdom of omniscience?

If the five poisons and their emotional problems
Did not manifest as a hundred and eighty understandings,
Who would have the wisdom of total omniscience dawn on them?

Sarva Jñāna Pañca Vidya A

If we do not understand that the three poisons
Are the three embodiments,
Who will have any recognition of the mighty one
Who has these three embodiments?

If we do not sever the roots
Of these self-originating three poisons,

A Tantra of the Great Perfection

What will we call the certitude
That is a recognition of the three embodiments?

If we do not know that an understanding of the three poisons
Comes to us by itself,
Who will these three embodiments teach the supreme symbols
On their own behalf?

If the three poisons do not manifest
As being pristinely self-liberated,
Who will use any warmth or validation
For the three bodies as a fruition?

Who is the mighty one that can delineate the boundaries
Of the seed of liberation
That is the Dharmakāya's fruition,
And is the seed for the two kinds of form embodiment?

If there were no three poisons,
What would be the validity of the three embodiments?
If there were no flashing,
There would be no mighty one
Who had the two embodiments.

If we did not have an eye
For which the flashing is like an illusion,
We would not have the seed
For the omniscience of the Sambhogakāya.

We see the illusion as being fivefold,
And although it appears in our domain,
We see its flashing with an illusory eye.

The thirty-two supreme markings may be visible,
But they are made into sixty-four vowel letters.
They are visible so that they can be used for a path.
These are the eighty-two exemplary features.

The forty-two consonants manifest as our base, path, and fruit.
We conjoin them
So that there are five aspects to the appearance of their virtues.

Our hair is black like a bee.
We see that our true nature is empty.
Our nails are very red,
But we see
That our compassion is an illusion.

Our teeth and fangs are white,
But we see that their essence is an illusion.
Our bodies are hidden,
Like Nyagrodha Bodhi Trees,
But we see their virtues
As being illusions.
Our markings and exemplary features are visible,
But we see our good works as being illusions.

Rays of light sink into our hearts,
And rays of light shine out from our hearts.
Wisdom dawns on us as a visible light.
Five lights form the appearance of our realm.
The light rays of effulgent happiness
Manifest as a brilliantly shining compassion.

A body that is like an illusion
Is a body that is like a rainbow.
If it did not flash,
The seeds of our Sambhogakāya would be lost.

So he spoke.

From the Tantra on the Non-duality of the Gods and the Demons, this is chapter eight: A Description of the Dharmakāya's Blessings upon the Sambhogakāya.

A DESCRIPTION OF
THE BLESSINGS OF THE DHARMAKĀYA
AND THE RECOGNITION OF THE DHARMAKĀYA
IN THE SIX CLASSES OF LIVING THINGS

Then the most pure one exclaimed:

Listen,
Dharma Mati,
You!

On the leaf of a *krishi* apple,
There is a lotus with a thousand petals.
There miraculously appears
An embodiment of compassion,
A holder of five illusions.

The blissful zombie[31] has emerged!
He teaches the way compassion manifests
To the mightiest of the gods, Śakra,[32]
And to many among the children of the gods.

He makes a blessing for every language
When he gives his explanations:
The languages of the gods and of the nagas,

---

[31] Ro langs bde ba. This was the birth-name of Garab Dorje, believed to be the founder of the Great Perfection transmission in our world.
[32] An epitaph for Indra.

The languages of the ghouls[33] and of the rakṣasas,[34]
And of the Asuras,
The living beings that are human,
The elementals,
And also the non-human beings.[35]

He has taught them.
He is teaching them.
He will teach them.

In that time,
And at that moment,
Through the compassionate blessings of the Nirmaṇakāya,
From the forest groves that are for the public,
Where there are fruit trees,
The sound of the totality of this Dharma
Is broadcast.

It is spoken out in the language of the gods,
But everyone hears it in their own language.
This is an indication that one language covers them all,
And is to be explained using the analogy
That there is an overabundance of transmissions that are twisted.[36]

If we do not understand how a wrathful face
May turn into a Nirmaṇakāya,
Who will be the mighty one that is born miraculously?

Who would it be that would gain certitude from a Dharma lecture?
Who would we teach the blessings, the warmth, and the validations?
Who would manifest the supreme signs of being blessed?
Who would get the result of being a Nirmaṇakāya?

If there were no flashing,
What would the virtues of a Nirmaṇakāya be?
What would it be that might be called:
"A magnificent method for working on knowledge."

---

[33] Grul bum
[34] Srin po
[35] Mi ma yin
[36] dGu po rgyud mangs

The Gods and the Demons Are Not Two

The six classes of living things do not flash,
So who would hope for a seed of freedom from them?

Who is the mighty one that has a knowledge of wisdom?
Who has certitude, warmth, and validation?

For whom will the fruition of self-liberated flashing come to pass?
Who will be the mighty one
That has cleared away both darkness and depression?

If the six classes of living beings were not sleeping in stupidity
Who would be the mighty one who has certitude
With regard to the instructions on sleeping in dhyāna meditation?

What will we call our lack of depression,
Our pristine awareness,
Or the degree of our warmth?
To whom will we give the supreme sign of self-luminous wisdom?

In our self-liberating stupidity
We have lost the fruits of the Dharmakāya.
For those who would hear
The all-encompassing Dharmakāya,
The instructions on the dhyāna of sleep are dear.

If we do not know the instructions
For suppressing false ideas about sleep,
We will not have any method by which
To apprehend our warmth and validations.
So if we lack a core
That is self-originating stupidity,
There will be no way for us
To manifest the self-originating Dharmakāya.

If stupidity does not manifest as self-liberating,
We will not be freed from stupidity by meditating.
If stupidity does not manifest as self-liberating,
It will be difficult for the self-evident Dharmakāya
To join into any equality with the four times.

So he spoke.

From the Tantra on the Non-duality of the Gods and the Demons this is chapter nine: A Description of the Blessings of the Dharmakāya and the Recognition of the Dharmakāya in the Six Classes of Living Things.

RECOGNITION OF THE SAMBHOGAKĀYA

Then the most pure one exclaimed:

Listen,
O Mightiest of Gods,
You!

Be without attachments for the six classes of sentient beings.

Who will be the one who is mighty
Over both distraction and wildness in their dhyāna meditation?

If we do not have a core
That liberates lust and hatred into their own place
What is it that we call:
"The instructions for giving birth to certitude
Regarding the Sambhogakāya"?
Who will establish a measure for the warmth
Of self-liberating lust and hatred?
To whom will we teach the great indicators
For pristine dhyāna meditation?

We have lost the seeds of freedom
That belong to the perfect Sambhogakāya.

If we do not have a core
In which our lust and hatred are liberated into their own place,
Who will have a recognition of the perfect Sambhogakāya?

If we do not have a core
In which our thoughts are self-originating and self-liberating
What sort of thing would a recognition
Of the knowledge of the Sambhogakāya be?

If we do not have a core
In which wildness and distraction move into self-liberation,
We destroy the seeds of the Sambhogakāya's freedom
By holding onto the subtle dhyāna that is in our minds.

If we do not have a core
In which subjects and objects are pristine,
To what will we attach the definition of a Sambhogakāya?

The Sambhogakāya appears as many things,
There within the circle of the self-evident great perfection.
Its embodiment is a self-originating,
Uncontrived, and pristine embodiment.
The Sambhogakāya is the best of them all!

It appears to us as being five self-originating Nirmaṇakāyas.
This is a magnificent vision,
A great clarity.
Light of a multitude of colors blazes.
We take on an embodiment that is like a magical illusion.

One body encompasses all things.
This is a self-evident body.
It is pervasive in being the five self-originating Great Ones.
Our ideas are self-liberating.
No matter how they manifest
They are transparent.

The embodiment of expertise,
Which is a net of magical illusions,
And the embodiment of self-appearance,
Which is entirely pure of all filth,
Are not to be confused.

Our self-luminousness is a compassion that has no measure.
The primary embodiment of the self-originating self-appearance
That works toward the destruction of the nets there are in our lives

Is a pervasive spirit,[37]
A spirit of five wisdoms.

The five bodies of the Buddhas
Are self-originating.
This self-evidence
Is not something we work towards or seek.
It dawns upon us!

E Ma Ho!
Kāya Trila Eka Prasara |
Dhatu Jñāna Bodhicitta Praña Cakṣu Pañca Rasayana Mamaki A |

O Bodhisattvas,
O Mightiest of Gods, Śakra,[38]
O Entourage of Gods and Servants:
Do not panic!
Do not be afraid!
Hold this in your heart for good!

The Sambhogakāya of self-evident understanding,
The Sambhogakāya that is the origin of compassion,
The Sambhogakāya that is generally pervasive,
The Sambhogakāya that is a vajra dominion,
The Sambhogakāya that is a light made of delusional visions,
And the perfect Sambhogakāya that is a manifest appearance:
All of these share the sound: "Sambhogakāya,"
But there are great differences.

The appearance of flashing lights,
The illusory appearances made by distortions of the flashing,
The self-evident two-pointedness of flashing wisdom,
The self-evident and self-liberating flashing,
And the unpredictable flashing
That comes from failure to recognize the flashing:
If we do not know the time
For the flashing of a light,
It will be difficult for there to be a border
Between Buddhas and sentient beings.

---

[37] Khyab bdag
[38] This is a name for Indra

A Tantra of the Great Perfection

On the borderlands of the light,
In the common ground,
Our senses,
And a vision of the triple mind,[39]
Are dear.

If the flashing does not manifest as a delusion,
It will be difficult to measure the time
During which delusions will be self-liberating.

If subjects and objects did not manifest
Even after the flashing,
It would be difficult to measure the time
In which wisdom becomes self-evident.

If the flashing were not unpredictable,
It would be difficult for a predictable wisdom to dawn on us.
If good understandings and bad understandings
Were not flashing,
It would be difficult to finish with measuring
The equanimity that is not an understanding.

If they did not flicker in a subtle kind of flashing
It would be difficult to cut through delusions.
If the flashing of a triple mind did not manifest,
It would be difficult to finish measuring
The three kinds of understandings.

If the flashing of rays did not flicker forth,
It would be difficult for the three embodiments of compassion
To appear.

If there were not any flashing that was very course,
It would be very difficult for the five poisons to be self-liberating.
If a multitude of entities were not flashing
It would be extremely difficult for their designators to be self-liberating.

If the flashing did not flicker in cooperation with sound,
It would be difficult to close the crevasses
That are the six classes of living beings.

---

[39] Yid gsum

The Gods and the Demons Are Not Two

If we do not cease measuring the flashing,
It will be difficult to cut through the roots
Of lives that are made out of heaps.[40]
If there is no recognition after the flash,
It will be extremely difficult to offer up a supported life.

If we do not understand that there is flashing within light,
It will be extremely difficult to discontinue the life we are supporting.

The mind, the flashing, and the light are a triad.
If we do not know how to recognize
Something that is self-evident
It will be difficult for us to cut through the three realms[41]
At their roots.
If an indivisible self-luminescence does not dawn on us,
It will be difficult to cut through the three existences[42]
At their roots.

If the flashing does not manifest as self-liberating,
It will be difficult to cut through ignorance
At the roots.
If a lucidity does not dawn on us after the flash,
It will be extremely difficult to see the face of the Buddha.

If the foundational circle[43] were not flashing,
It would be extremely difficult to deplete the pristine.

If this does not dawn on us as being self-evident after it flashes,
It will be extremely difficult to be liberated by doing meditation.
If our lives have not been cut off at the root
After the flashing,
It will be extremely difficult to evade the pits of samsara.

If we do not have a core of brilliance
After the flashing,
It will be extremely difficult
To use a seal to stop the three existences.

---

[40] Sanskrit Skandha, Tibetan Phung po.
[41] The realms of desire, form, and formlessness.
[42] Below the ground, on the ground, and in the sky.
[43] gZhi yi thig le

If we do not understand that there is an inner dawning
After the flashing,
It will be extremely difficult to open the eye that is ignorant.

If we do not believe that things we do not understand are flashing,
It will be extremely difficult for wisdom to dawn on us.
It will be extremely difficult for us to stamp our seal
Upon the mouth of the womb.

If the absence of any object does not dawn on us
After the flashing,
It will be difficult for those who hold onto objects
And travel through levels
To become Buddhas.

If a path did not appear to us
After the flashing,
It would be difficult to study the five paths.

If self-perfection does not dawn on us
After the flashing,
It will be extremely difficult for us
To gather up our two accumulations.

If stainlessness did not dawn on us
After the flashing,
It would be extremely difficult for us
To clean away our obstructions.

If we do not cut off the one who travels
At the roots,
There will not be a time in which we surmount the levels.

If we do not understand that the five paths are flashing
It will be difficult to finish with measuring
The time periods for the five paths.

If the flashing did not manifest as non-dual
It would be difficult for our two accumulations
To be perfected into one.

If flashing does not manifest as stainless,
It will be difficult to know the measures

For our cleansing away our obstructions.

This is easy because it is difficult,
This flashing eye!
It is the flashing eye that cuts through the roots.
It surmounts the levels.
It studies the paths.
It completes the great accumulations.
It clears away our obstructions.
Buddhahood dawns on us.

Those who practice all kinds of things,
While they refer to the time,
Are like those who would also be done with measuring the sky.
It is difficult to teach them.

So he spoke.

From the Tantra on the Non-duality of the Gods and the Demons, this is chapter ten: Recognition of the Sambhogakāya.

THE NIRMAṆAKĀYA APPEARS IN THE CIRCLE OF THE LIGHT OF AWARENESS

Then again the most pure one exclaimed:

On the summit of a Jambu Priśa
He gave instructions
To his most precious minister of war:

If we have no habitual tendencies,
The Nirmaṇakāya will not manifest.

There are the habitual tendencies
Of the light that cuts through to the highest limits,
The habitual tendencies that bring together the white and the red seed,
The habitual tendencies of the names
And the objects we attribute to them,
And the self-liberating habitual tendencies
By which we compassionately train living beings.
These share the words "habitual tendencies,"
But there are great differences.

The roots of our habitual tendencies and our attachments
Are of two sorts.
They are both subsumed within the five poisons.
If we do not cut through them at the roots,
There will not be a time in which
We have cut through the roots of the five poisons.

That is the instruction that the All Good One gave,
And on that occasion,
At that time,
From the top of that Jambu Priśa tree,
A turquoise cuckoo sang out three times, singing:

Budha Cakṣu Ratna Phala A |

Then singing:

  Lokaca Avyiddhakhya |

Then singing:

  Karma Budha | Vajra Budha | Tathāgate Budhade |
Padma Budha Cakṣu Phala Prasara |

Those are the words it sang out three times.

All the Bodhisattvas who dwell within the realms of the world gathered.
There was the king of the gods, Brahma.
There was the king of the asuras, Druma.
There was the king of the humans, Dharma Ratsa.[44]
There was the king of the animals, the Steadfast Lion.
There was the king of the hungry ghosts, the Snake-headed Belly Crawler.
There was the king of the hells, the Three Skulls and Staffs,
And there were others:
There were the eight congregations of gods and rākṣasa demons.[45]
There was a gathering of representatives of the six classes of living beings.

All of them circumambulated the turquoise cuckoo seven times each. Then they said:

We beg you to speak to us in our own language!

---

[44] Probably a corrupt form of Dharma Raja.
[45] Srin po

So the turquoise bird transformed into a beautiful little child, and said:

Let delight for me be born in you!
Through a multitude of manifest languages
I will make this meaningful.

This is also what he will say.

Then a multitude of light rays beamed out from this child's heart into the ten directions, and there appeared an uninterrupted mass of light in five colors.

From the circle of the light of awareness there miraculously appeared a Nirmaṇakāya that is made out of light, and an immeasurable number of Nirmaṇakāyas did appear.

The *Lokarajas* who were gathered there
Were most delighted,
And were very pleased,
And because they were so pleased,
They offered up their jewelry.

The king of the gods took Śakra,
The mightiest of the gods,
And in the land of the gods
He granted him an empowerment,
Using seven precious things to symbolize the empowerment.
He also granted the outer, inner, and hidden empowerments.

For stainlessness and purity
There was the empowerment of the washing vessel.

To perfect the accumulation of pleasures
There was the empowerment of the seven precious things.

To perfect the accumulation of wisdom
There was the empowerment of the precious jewel.

To perfect the power of our vehicle
There is the elephant empowerment.

To be possessed of the power of miracles
There is the empowerment of the precious horse.

To perfect our three splendors
There is the empowerment of the precious minister of war.

To translate a multitude of words
There is the empowerment of the precious minister.

To unite everyone
On top of a single throne,
There is the empowerment of the precious king.

To make a variety of things happen
There is the empowerment of the precious queen.

To bring everything together
There is the empowerment of the seven jewels
Of the gods from the realms of desire.

In a mere moment,
Instantaneously,
He granted them empowerment in full,
And the mightiest of the gods Śakra
Was liberated from his station.

It was on this occasion,
The time that the Nirmaṇakāya appeared in the abode of the gods,
That he gave the gods of the three realms
The symbols for the empowerments,
The implements,
And the substances for the empowerments.
So the name Giver of Hundreds: Śakra
Was given to him.

So he spoke.

From the Tantra on the Non-duality of the Gods and the Demons, this is chapter eleven: The Nirmaṇakāya appears in the Circle of the Light of Awareness.

THE REVELATION THAT VEMACITRA IS A NIRMAṆAKĀYA

Then the most pure one exclaimed:

Listen,
Vajra Dharma Mati,
You!

From out of the circle of the light of awareness
The king of the Asuras Vemacitra
Met with a company of Asuras
At the roots of the Jambu Priśa tree.

There was Camphor, the king of medicine,
Sandalwood, the king of the trees,
Magnet, the king of the stones,
Peacock, the king of the birds,
And Crocodile, the king of the animals.

He performed the granting of the empowerment
For all of them.

Camphor is a spontaneously formed substance.
The King of Awareness is a spontaneously formed empowerment.

Sandalwood, with the power of its scent,
Is a substance used in the imparting of the empowerment

By the three bodies,
On their own behalf.

Just as the king of the stones,
The magnet,
Draws in iron,
This empowerment draws in every good thing.

Just as the peacock eats poison,
The five poisons impart the best empowerments.

Just as crocodiles do not appear in the desert,
When we acquire the mountain empowerment[46]
We are empowered not to have to wander in samsara.

He imparted on them the implements of empowerment
Belonging to the Asuras,
The symbols for the empowerment,
And the real things used for the empowerment,
In full.

Their virtues appeared by themselves,
With no problems.

Those who did not understand the five doors of entry
Were taught the empowerment on the cycle of offering the chakras,[47]
And the empowerment of entering the mandala[48]
As collective empowerments.

Now there are the specific teachings on the mandala:

The basis of all things
Is an extensive mandala.
A method for entering it
Has not been recognized.

The mind is a mandala of peace.
The method for entering it
Is its self-originating chakra.

---

[46] Ri dbang
[47] 'Khor lo mchod bskor
[48] dKyil 'khor 'jug pa

The five doors
Are a mandala of real practice.
The method for entering them
Is the cakras of our consciousnesses.

The consciousness of our bodies
Is a fierce mandala.
The method for entering it
Is the mandala in which we see god.

The consciousness of our minds
Is the mandala for the empowerment.
The method for entering it
Is a mandala of light.

Each of these, in turn,
Is constructed out of five mandalas in full completion.
The method for entering them
Is to be complete in each of the five.

When we enter the mandala of the Victorious One,
We will need the flowers of the clear light of omniscience.
The holy implement is the wisdom of the dominion of the Dharma.
At the moment we receive
The imparting of the empowerment
Into a non-dual and stainless body,
We are instantaneously perfected.
The result is a pristine circle.
Its virtue is omniscience.

When we enter the mandala of peace,
We will need the flowers of self-originating clear light.
The moment we receive the imparted empowerment,
A body of stainless wisdom,
We will instantaneously be a self-liberating body.
The result is a pristine wisdom.
Its virtue is that it is a self-originating wisdom.

When we enter the mandala for the empowerment,
We will need the flowers of stainless clear light.
For the implements for the empowerment
We will need a totally perfected wisdom.

The method for imparting it
Is a body of the clear light of wisdom.
The moment we receive it,
We are instantaneously born into a self-perfected body.
The result is a pristine awareness
That is not a Dharma.
Its virtue is that it is a self-aware wisdom.

When we enter the mandala of a real practice,
We will need the flowers of the stainless clarity of appearance.
For the implements for the empowerment
We will need self-originating wisdom.
For the method of imparting it
We will need a stainless clarity of appearances.
The moment we receive it,
We will instantly have self-luminous bodies.
The result is a pristine non-duality.
Its virtue is that it is a totally pure realm.

When we enter the mandala of wrath,
We will need the flowers of self-liberating clear light.
For the implements for the empowerment
We will need a vigorous wisdom.
For the method of empowerment,
There is the body of the inner clarity of wisdom.
At the moment we receive it,
We instantaneously become self-originating bodies.
The result is a body of wisdom that sees god.
Its virtue is that it is self-liberated from form.

The eye is a symbol for the empowerment into a real practice.
The ear is a symbol for the empowerment into peace.
The nose is a symbol for the empowerment into prosperity.
The mouth is a great symbol of power.
The lower doors are symbols for the empowerment into wrath.

The connections between analogies and symbols,
And the connections between symbols and meanings,
Are dear.
All of them are subsumed within each of them.

Five mandalas are perfected in the eye.
White perfects the mandala of peace.

Yellow perfects the mandala of prosperity,
Red perfects the mandala of power.
Dark blue perfects the mandala of wrath.
Green perfects the mandala of real practice.

These manifestations are the mandalas of the body.
The five lights from a concave crystal
Perfect the mandala of the perfect Sambhogakāya.

Through the blazing of the jeweled *citta*,
A magnificent wisdom of awareness
Is perfected.

When we recognize the three bodies in our hearts,
Our construction of the three mandalas
Will be perfected in this.
Its virtues are the two effulgencies of wisdom.
This is the perfection of the triple construct mandala.

These are the teachings on the reality of the Nirmaṇakāya:
They will be evident to an eye of jewels.

The Sambhogakāya is hidden in the base,
But it is present in the jewel nerves.[49]
The Nirmaṇakāya is present on its own behalf,
But it dwells in a heart of jewels.[50]
A fitting analogy for their recognition,
Is that a jewel crystal is pristine.
This is a fitting analogy
For the recognition of the Nirmaṇakāya.

It is within it that the light is present.
This is a fitting analogy
To establish that the Sambhogakāya is within the base.

It appears that minute tendons[51]
Come out of it.
This is a fitting analogy for the emergence of the Nirmaṇakāya.

---

[49] Rin chen rtsa
[50] Rin chen snying
[51] rGyus phran

A Tantra of the Great Perfection

The dawning of a light in a crystal jewel
Is a fitting analogy for the mandala of the Sambhogakāya.

The reality of the *bardo*
Is a fitting analogy for clear light.
The five mandalas are perfected within it.
Its virtues dawn upon us,
For the mandala of expansiveness is perfect.

This is the spontaneously created mandala
In which everything is created within ourselves.

So he spoke.

The Asuras came to be fully liberated.

It is because he teaches that everything is in a pattern,[52]
But that within it there is nothing there,
So it is fine,[53]
And that he is partial[54]
To the coordination of analogies, symbols, meanings,
And associated topics.
This is why he is called Vemacitra.[55]

So it is said.

From the Tantra on the Non-duality of the Gods and the Demons, this is chapter twelve: The Revelation that Vemacitra is a Nirmaṇakāya.

---

[52] Thags
[53] bZangs
[54] Ris
[55] Thags bzangs ris. It is likely that these lines were added by Tibetans as an explanation for the Tibetan translation of the name Vemacitra, the King of the Asuras.

SHARING THE TASTE OF BEING
AN EXTERNAL FURY

Then the most pure one exclaimed:

Listen,
Vajra Dharma Mati,
You!

The Blessed One,
The Muni Siddhartha,
Manifested himself
From out of the circle of the light of awareness.

He was the foremost leader
Of living beings who have two feet.
He expounded on what is properly meaningful.
He explained the meanings of the symbols,
And what is attached to them.

When he saw us at the Jambu Prikṣa tree,
He began to teach us the basic ground for our delusions.

In a magnificent abode
That was spontaneously made manifest,
Without limiting any vastness,
Or falling into any bias:
For when we do not limit a vastness,

We do not fall into any bias,
And when we do not fall into any bias,
We do not limit any vastness.

So we possess an eye
That is spontaneously made manifest.

For humans,
Gods and demons are topics that give birth to ideas.
At first,
A reckoning of the basic ground is dear.

In a basic recognition of the triad:
Causes, conditions, and entities,
We will share their taste,
And our sorrows will have been brilliantly purified.
This is the supreme path of freedom!

The six Maras that are generally pervasive,
And specifically the four classes of Maras,
Are Maras of true essence:
They destroy everything without feeling anything.
Demons are obstacles that get in our way.

The five aspects of our own foundation
Become foundations for the five kinds of demons.
The works of the demons and rākṣasas
Are to be comprehensively pacified.

This is a time when demons and rākṣasas
Cannot be distinguished from among the humans.
Brahma has descended upon or touched on
The foundation of all things
In this way.

There are three kinds of hermaphrodite:
The analogy, the symbol, and the meaning.
They are the analogies, symbols, and applications
For the mind.

The flickering in our minds
Is the spirit of a demon.
The five lights dawn on us

The Gods and the Demons Are Not Two

As being the conditions for the five kinds of demons.

It is by the green,
That demons and rākṣasas
Are to be distinguished among humans.

The great light that discerns all things
Has light rays that appear in everything.
She is called the Goddess Keeper of Light Rays,
Mārīcī.

She has five demons that are material beings.
Their flesh and blood is actually born from out of light.
These demons that are material beings
Appear among us,
And illuminate our eight classes of consciousness.[56]

The so-called eight consortiums of gods and demons
Is a description of material beings and what we attach to them.

Within the base of all things
There are the Maras[57] of the eyes,
The kings[58] of the ears,
The spirits[59] of the nose,
And the monsters[60] of the tongue.
The malevolent demons[61] of our bodies,
The planetary influences,[62]
Nagas,[63]
Crones,[64]
And an assortment of gods and demons,
And they have matured into being something real.

Now I will explain what it means to infiltrate and overthrow them,
Which is something that is inconceivable to the demons.

---

[56] rNam shes tshogs brgyad
[57] bDud
[58] rGyal po. This is a class of demon.
[59] rMu
[60] bTsan
[61] gNod sbyin
[62] Yid gza'
[63] kLu
[64] Ma mo

A Tantra of the Great Perfection

These demons have degraded themselves into being Maras.
There are also the ones that are called: "Mara demons."[65]
There is even one that is called: "The Great Mara of Us All."[66]
In summary,
There are eight kinds of rākṣasa demon.[67]

A rākṣasa demon has one eye,
A red face,
And is renowned for what is called: "The Nine Forms."[68]
We penetrate through these nine doors,
So we call them: "The doors for entering into the demonic."

To sum this up:
The five kinds of demons
Enter through the five doors.

Even more briefly:
The root demons are subsumed in being
The demons of our designations and of our attachments.

If we do not understand
That the ones who are revolting
Are the demons,
There will not come a time of freedom
For the demons!

We must work toward freedom for the demons!
We must share in the taste of the experience
Of being external furies.[69]

There are three ways in which we share in the taste
Of being a fury:
The contrived method uses dependencies and connections
Between ritual implements;
Through meditating on a god we are calmed;
Through recognition there is a shared taste.

---

[65] 'Dre bdud
[66] Kun kyi bdud chen
[67] 'Dre srin
[68] rNam pa dgu
[69] 'Byung po, an elemental spirit.

These are what we call:
"The subjugation of all the furies."

The method for exorcising furies
Is the three recognitions.
These are the three:
Designations, attachments, and non-duality.

The contrived method uses implements
And the three dependent connections:
The soul-stone,[70] the soul-abode,[71]
And the abode of the soul's structure.[72]

The demons, the Maras, and the ways that they harm us are a triad.
The indications of harm, the methods of exorcism, and the time to expel them are a triad.
Contrived methods, the degree to which they are contrived, and the time in which they are contrived are a triad.
The place we enter, the time we enter, and the time we emerge are a triad.
Demons, humans, and rākṣasas are a triad.
Divisions, dividing, and the time in which we divide are a triad.
Designations, our using them to divide things, and the senses are a triad.
Virtues, fruitions, and a place that has been liberated are a triad.
The foundation of the demons, inner upheavals among the demons, and the degree of them are a triad.
Results, ascertained knowledge, and qualifications are a triad.
Encounters, meetings, and schedules are a triad.
The senses, ascertained knowledge, and boundaries are a triad.
The ability to handle conditions, warmth, and signs are a triad.
Results, qualifications, and awakening are a triad.
Our foundation, causes and conditions, and real awakening are a triad.
Designations, attachments, and troubled awakening are a triad
The senses that are awoken, the knowledge that is ascertained, and the ability to handle conditions are a triad.
Results, qualifications, and our degree of awakening are a triad.
The base, the path, and the fruit
Are a triad of sacrificial grounds.
The ground of sacrifice, the time of sacrifice, and the degree of sacrifice

---

[70] bLa rdo
[71] bLa gnas
[72] bLa rten gnas

are a triad.

The senses, the knowledge of certitude, and the ability to handle conditions are a triad.

The Sage's fruition, his degree of warmth, and his signs are a triad.

His qualifications, the degree to which they are revealed, and the time in which they are set free are a triad.

The senses that are set free, the ability to handle conditions, and the knowledge of certitude are a triad.

The time of our fruition, our qualifications, and our own place are subsumed into a triad.

So he spoke.

From the Tantra on the Non-duality of the Gods and the Demons, this is chapter thirteen: Sharing the Taste of Being an External Fury.

SHARING THE TASTE OF THE DISEASES
OF INTERMITTENT ATTACHMENT AND HATRED

Then the most pure one exclaimed:

Listen,
Vajra Dharma Mati,
You!

We must be liberated from the diseases of attachment and hatred,
So I will teach you to share the taste
Of the diseases of attachment and hatred.

To do this,
I will start by teaching you the basis for disease.

Five diseases are formed within the foundation.
They are spontaneously formed within the foundation.
The foundation does not stop them,
So there are a variety of diseases.

Their cause is that we retain them after they flash.
Their conditions are that we take them to be diseases.

Out of the light that there is between us,
Who will be attached to whom?
When we are attached to the light,
We give birth to hatred.

When we do not understand non-duality
We give birth to stupidity.

This being so,
Our attachment and hatreds have actually matured
Into our physical bodies,
And we are tormented by the five illnesses
Which are combinations of them,
As well as an essential illness,
Making six.

Our essential illness has two aspects:
There is the illness of the mind that makes us age,
And the illness from being embodied that makes us die.
These two are combined
Into an inconceivable number of conditional illnesses.

Illnesses from the cold are of five kinds.
Even those who cling to reason
Accept that on the trunk of the twenty-five illnesses
Each of them has a spontaneously realized Dharma.
When they are combined,
Disease is what happens.

Their occurrence has the same taste as a battle.
Contrivance in the use of implements.
Meditation on a deity,
And recognition,
Share the same taste.

First, we recognize the basic ground.
We will come to understand the basis for the disease,
Which will show us the time in which to stop it.

We will then understand the symptoms of the disease.
This will show us the strength of the illness at its worst.
Then we will know the method of treatment
And the methods for exorcising it.
A battle among the elements
Is a conditional disease.

The Gods and the Demons Are Not Two

I will teach you the recognition of the unborn.
When we are held by heat,
We encounter an inner clarity.
We encounter a clear light.

When we are held by winds,
We encounter a pristine reality.
When we are held by bile
We encounter self-liberation.
When we are held by gatherings,
We encounter a lack of location.

If the head is ill,
Green draws it out.
If the throat is ill,
Dark green draws it out.
If our heart is ill,
We use yellow on the upper part of the body
To draw it out.

If the disease is in the lower part of the body,
In the capillaries[73] of the kidneys,
We use dark blue on it,
For this will expunge it.

If the soles of our feet or our knees are ill,
We use white on them,
As this will expunge it.

These are the methods and the expungings.
They are avenues of treatment.

Treatment is carried out
As a door to stainlessness,
As a door to pristine awareness,
As a door for the red,
As a hole for the life-force,
As a door for the vajra,
And as a door for the lotus.

---

[73] rTsa khol ma

A Tantra of the Great Perfection

The navel opens out at the door of the lotus.

If the heart is not well,
It is in our eyes.
If the lungs are not well,
It is in the nose.
If the kidneys are not well,
It is hidden.
If the liver is not well
It is in the mouth.
If the gall is not well,
It is in the eyes.

Now we will share the taste of being a god.

When we are sick from the heat,
That is Akṣobhya.
When we are sick from the cold,
That is Amoghasiddhi.
When our gallbladder is ill,
That is Vairochana's embodiment.
If our phlegm is ill,
That is Ratnasambhava.
If our constitution is diseased,
That is Amitabha.

If we are sick with heat,
That is Mamaki.
If we are sick with cold,
That is the Lady of White Gown.[74]
If our gallbladder is diseased,
That is the Lady of Wealth's Dominion.[75]
If our phlegm is diseased,
That is Buddha Eyes.[76]
If our constitution is ill,
That is Tara.
Through these we share in the taste
Of being a god.

---

[74] Gos dkar mo
[75] dByings phyug ma
[76] Sangs rgyas spyan

The essence of illness is the illness of the mind.
If we do not distinguish our minds from our wisdom
It will be difficult to be free
From the sickness of death.

If we do not distinguish the two kinds of actual practice,
It will be difficult to be free
Of the disease of old age.

If we do not understand that the diseases are of a common flavor
It will be difficult to overcome the delusion of being sick.
If we do not cut through our delusions about disease at the roots,
It will be extremely difficult for us to experience a shared taste.

A mighty one who has shared the taste of the disease
Must use his mind.
The illness, in our ascertained knowledge, is pristine.

The time for battle
Is when we are able to handle the conditions.
The pain that is a sign of warmth is pristine.
The result of this is that the disease is self-liberating.

Our qualifications are things
That we will sacrifice for the future.

From the Tantra on the Non-duality of the Gods and the Demons this is chapter fourteen: Sharing the Taste of Diseases from Intermittent Attachment and Hatred.

SHARING A TASTE FOR IDEAS

Then the most pure one exclaimed:

Listen,
Vajra Dharma Mati,
You!

I will teach you the shared taste of intermittent ideas.

First I will teach you about the basis for our ideas.

Our ideas about the five poisons
Are fully present in our foundation.
Rage and ignorance are the basis of our ideas.
This is similar to the way in which camphor,
Being a medicine,
Is fully a poison.

Our ideas are completely present
In a foundation that is non conceptual,
But all of our emotions and ideas
Are delusions from their very foundation.

The cause of our ideas is a mental flickering.
Its conditions are that ignorance is born from light.
The appearance of the other is ignorance.

Self-originating ignorance has nine ways of grasping
In which non-dual ignorance is distorted into a multiplicity:

The ignorance of true essence,
The ignorance that is hidden and concealed,
The ignorance that is synchronously born,
The ignorance that is totally a designation,
The ignorance in which visible appearances are wrong,
The ignorance that does not extend into serving as a condition,
The ignorance in which causes and conditions are measured in time,
The ignorance that self-evidently guides us,
And the ignorance that controls us when we are open to it.

These are manifestations of our understandings as material things.
There are eighty thousand ideas and emotions.
They are summarized into the five emotions.[77]
All five of them are summarized into attachment and hatred.
Material things are the appearances of our delusions.

Now to share the taste of our thinking.

The equanimity of non-conceptuality is the Dharmakāya.
Ideas are the delusions of ignorance,
So I will teach you the method for combining recognition
With the three bodies:

When appearances are conceptualized,
I teach the recognition of non-conceptual awareness.
To the average,
I teach the Wheel of Clear Light.
To the rude,
I teach the Wheel of the Suppression of What is Wrong.

It is possible that the vastness of the sky
Turns out to be merely a canopy of appearances,
So I turn the wheel of the clear light of appearance.

I teach the recognition of self-evident awareness.
It will dawn upon you that appearances are self-liberating.
It is right when the self-liberation of appearances
Dawns on us

---

[77] Lust, hatred, stupidity, jealousy, and pride.

The Gods and the Demons Are Not Two

That we are obviously at our own doorway
Into an awareness of appearance.

It is like being a rainbow that melts into the sky.

In the state of awareness
Appearances are liberated.
Whatever we see
Is whatever we free.
This is the state of our awareness.

Self-origination, self-liberation, and the way these are combined
Are a triad.
Appearances are mixed in with awareness.
Awarenesses are mixed in with wisdom.
Wisdom is mixed into a circle.
This is the self-evident liberation of our senses.

A knowledge of certitude is self-evident to our awareness.
Its validation is that it is a unified circle.
Its degree of warmth is the clear light of our awareness.
The best of signs is a vision that has no object.
The result is a pristine circle.
Its virtue is that the circle is not a Dharma.

Compassion appears by itself,
And has no location.

So he spoke.

When we hold onto our minds while clamping our mouths,
It is possible that the heights of our vision be lost.
We must combine a clamped mouth with a loose mouth.
Our six gatherings[78] spin in a wheel of clear light.

The six gatherings are mighty,
And are self-liberating.
Our consciousness is the certitude of clear light.
A pristine non-grasping is our conviction.
The five kinds of good things we desire

---

[78] Tshogs drug. The six kinds of consciousness: Vision, hearing, tasting, smelling, feeling, and thinking.

Are our ability to handle conditions.

Attachments and hatreds
Are the signs that there is warmth on Mt. Meru.
With attachment,
The things we desire are liberated into their own place.
This is described as being the finest of results.
The six gatherings of good things are abundant.
The fitting analogy for this is that the sun rises.

So he spoke.

To combine a lose mouth with a clamped mouth,
We turn a wheel of flickering clear light.
The degree of its flashing
Is the force of the clear light.
The self-liberation of the flashing is our certitude.
The fresh awakening of the flashing is our conviction.
This flickering is able to handle conditions
Wherever it flashes.

The understanding that comes after the flashing
Is a sign of heat.
The white and black flashes are liberated into their own place.
The result is renowned to be the best.

The flashing forth of good things happens by itself.
A fitting analogy is that this resembles
A turbulence in the wind.

So he spoke.

Combination, mixture, and the amounts to be mixed are a triad.
Heat, signs, and sense organs are a triad.
Certitude, qualifications, and fitting analogies are a triad.
This is the recognition that comes from the general instructions.

So he spoke.

Now for the unmistaken recognition of the flashing.

We look at the flashing with a stare,
And see it with a stare.

The Gods and the Demons Are Not Two

When we finish,
Wisdom will dawn on us by itself.

The Dharmakāya has no location,
But it empties the realms of hell.
Do not blame the bat
For not offering praise to the garuda.

E Ma Ho!
It is self-originating!
It is self-liberating!
It wanders by itself.

The Dharmakāya has not found any place of refuge,
But hell itself cannot harm it.
It does not find a place to stretch its body in freedom,
But the lord of hell does not find any way to harm it.

When we hold the flashing in a stare,
Buddhahood dawns within us.

Lack of understanding,
Ignorance,
And samsara
Dawn upon us.
It is very difficult for something that dawns on itself
To understand its own core.

So he spoke.

Again he gave instructions:

If we do not divide darkness and appearance into two,
Who will appreciate the degree of warmth of our inner sinking?

If we do not divide the summer, winter, fall, and spring,
Who will hold to the rule of the year, month, and day?

If we do not establish the differences between the five kinds of disease,
What will we count on for life-giving medicinal compounds?

If we do not establish a difference
Between the demons and the rākṣasas,

We will have no method to recognize obstructions.

If we do not establish a difference between the gods and the demons,
What will we use as a method to attain siddhis?

If we do not divide Buddhas from sentient beings,
Who will exemplify the defiled and the undefiled?

If we do not divide subjects and objects into two,
To whom will we teach pristine non-duality?

If we do not divide appearances and the world into two,
To whom will we teach self-evident purity?

If we do not divide mind and wisdom,
To whom will we teach that the intellect and reality are not two?

If we do not divide the foundation of all things and the past,
Then what are our understandings and realizations for?

If we do not divide the primordial and knowledge,
To whom will we teach pristine wisdom?

If we do not divide habits and clingings,
To whom will we teach the way of the transfer of the body?[79]

If we do not divide attachment and hatred,
To whom will we teach about the delusions of the five poisons?

If we do not divide methods and wisdom,
To whom will we teach contact with the final instructions?

If we do not divide our eyes,
To whom will we teach the one eye of wisdom?

If we do not make a division among bodies,
To whom will we teach the leaving behind of a body?

If we do not establish a difference in hearts,
To whom will we teach about pristine non-duality?

---

[79] Lus kyi spo lugs

The Gods and the Demons Are Not Two

If we do not establish a difference in locations,
To whom will we teach pristine awareness that has no location?

If we do not establish differences in qualifications,
To whom will we teach about the pristine awareness
That is not a Dharma?

If we do not establish a difference in wisdoms,
To whom will we teach pristine wisdom?

So he spoke.

If we do not establish a distinction in the analogies,
To whom will we show a black jackal?

There are no benefits or damages
In either darkness or appearance.
If we do not teach that there are no benefits,
And that there are no damages,
To whom will we show
The private doorway of awareness?

So he spoke.

From the Tantra on the Non-duality of the Gods and the Demons, this is chapter fifteen: Sharing a Taste for Ideas.

SHARING THE TASTE OF BEING A SECRET AND UNSURPASSED DEITY

Then again the most pure one exclaimed:

Listen,
Vajra Dharma Mati,
You!

I will teach you to share the taste
Of being a secret and unexcelled deity.
Above all, this is our foundation for being a god.

I bow to the naturally and spontaneously realized deity!

Dewa Rāja Namo Pūja Ratna Karmma Budha Tathāgata Samudra Mahāguhya Ati Jñāna Patna Phala Cakra |

Through beginningless time,
There are the gods of spontaneously formed awareness,
The gods of intermittent causes and conditions
That form into clear light,
The gods of empowerment,
As well as the gods of the mandala,
The gods whose names are rude attributions,
And gods who take the form of illuminators
When we think of them in our minds.

A Tantra of the Great Perfection

Dewa Samādhi |
Pūja Māhaguhya Phala Phala |

The god of power is Amitabha.
The god of peace is Akṣobhya.
The god of wrath is Vairochana.
The god of prosperity is Ratnasambhava.
The god of real productivity is Amoghasiddhi.

These deities are the external *Dewa Rāja* gods.
The five colors are present in their eyes:
Dark blue,
White,
Yellow,
Poppy,
And green.
These are present without being mixed.

This is the empowerment for the perfection stage deity!
You have been imparted the empowerment of the self-liberating deity.

The pristine *cakṣu*[80] is the mighty Akṣobhya.
The clear light *cakṣu* is Amitabha.
The self-evident *cakṣu* is the person of Ratnasambhava.
The self-originating *cakṣu* is the great Amoghasiddhi.

The teachings on the five thrones for the symbols are that
They are upon the thrones of
A lion,
A peacock,
An elephant,
A horse,
And a garuda.

We do not meditate on a mandala for the five embodiments of wisdom.

This is the empowerment of perfection:

Ābeśa Tathāgata Jñāna Budha Ratna Pariśudhayā |

The empowerment is granted when we say this with our voices.

---

[80] The Sanskrit word for eye.

The foundation, the path, and real things are a triad.
There are three instructions for their recognition.

The king of empowerments is the wisdom empowerment.
In a single instant,
We are perfected.

So he spoke.

From the Tantra on the Non-duality of the Gods and the Demons, this is chapter sixteen: Sharing the Taste of Being a Secret and Unsurpassed Deity.

THE TIME OF
THE DESTRUCTION OF THE WORLD

Then the most pure one exclaimed:

Listen,
Vajra Dharma Mati,
You!

I will teach you to share the taste of being an element.

In the beginning
There was a spontaneously formed foundation for all things.
The five elements presided,
From the very start.

To make things move there was the foundation of wind.
To make things grow there was the foundation of earth.
To make things ripen there was the foundation of fire.
To make things congeal there was the foundation of water.
To open up the vastness of space there was the foundation of the sky.

When we put all these together,
There are four great elements.
When these great elements shift,
Our awareness flashes.
This is the apparent condition for the five lights.

Emerging from out of this foundation,
There is a foundation of light.
From out of a vision of radiant clear light,
The inner elements are distorted
Into being the five kinds of things that are within our bodies.
The secret elements are distorted into being the flashing.
The external elements are distorted into being five kinds of object.
This is the way that we engage the elements.

Now I will publish the methods for exorcising them.

When we recognize that forms are flashes,
We may even share the taste of being one of the five great ones.

To share the taste of being earth,
Teach awareness.
To share the taste of being water,
Illuminate awareness.
To share the taste of being fire,
Ripen awareness.
To share the taste of being sky,
Let pristine awareness dawn.
To share the taste of being wind,
Let breathlessness dawn.

If we do not know how to share the taste of being the water
We may be deviating toward a severing of our awareness.
If we do not know how to share the taste of being the earth,
We may be deviating toward a change in our awareness.
If we do not know how to share the taste of being fire,
We may be deviating toward the existence of objects
And those who have them.
If we do not know how to share the taste of being the wind,
We may be deviating toward a cleansing of our breath.
If we do not know how to share the taste of being the sky,
We may be deviating
Into the existence of something that is permanent and constant.

If we do not know how to share the taste of being the great elements
We may be deviating into the extremes of the lesser elements.
When we share the taste of being an external element,
We will need our senses to make four kinds of recognition.

The Gods and the Demons Are Not Two

For the self-liberation of the elements,
We will need certitude.
We will need a conviction that the five elements are self-appearing.
We will need to be able to handle the conditions
Under which the five elements are clear light.

We will need to cast off our attachments and clingings,
And to have signs of warmth.
We will need to stamp the five elements that are our results
With seals.

The good things that are to come are five.
Those that are past are five.

A fitting analogy is that this resembles ice and water.

The thing we call: "Sharing the taste of being an inner element"
Is that all five elements are present within our bodies.

The shared taste of being aware is extremely dear.
The five elements in our senses,
Are our attachments, their destruction, and their emptiness.

The destroyers of Mr. Meru are embodied beings.
The destroyers of the four continents are the four deeps.
The destroyer of the outer islands is one with eight feet.
The destroyers of the seven lakes
Are the seven groups.
That destroy seven mountains
In seven nations.

The destroyer of the great forests
Is at the root of life's existence.
The destroyer of the four forests
Is the four branch nerves.[81]
The eight nerves of the moving stars
Are on the spine.
The destroyer of the sun and the moon
Is our two eyes.
The destroyer of the eight planets

---

[81] rTsa

Is our eight gatherings.[82]
The destroyer of the nine joints
Is at our core.
Nine refers to our nine doors on their own behalf.

The destruction of the earth is flesh.
The destruction of fire is loss of heat.
The destruction of wind is the loss of our complexion.
The destruction of water is the aging of our bodies.
The destruction of the sky is the shimmering in our minds.
The destruction of the great elements is the absence of any flashing.
This is a summary of the destruction of the elements.

The five great ones
Are subsumed within the five elements.
As an analogy,
They are like magnets that pick up iron.

So he spoke.

From the Tantra on the Non-duality of the Gods and the Demons, this is chapter seventeen: The Time of the Destruction of the World.

---

[82] Tshogs brgyad. This refers to the eight types of consciousness as described by the Yogacara school.

LIVING IN A PEACEFUL ABIDING

Then again the most pure one exclaimed:

Listen,
Vajra Dharma Mati,
You!

After the destruction there is emptiness.
I will explain.

When the earth is destroyed
There will be no support structure.
When the wind is destroyed
There will be no motion.
When the fire is destroyed
There will be nothing to make things ripen.
When the water is destroyed
There will be nothing to make them coalesce.
When the sky is destroyed
There will be no moving stars,
No planets,
No sun and no moon.

The sky that encompasses all things,
The sky that is used to make fitting analogies,
The sky that is a self-originating reality,
And the sky of true essence
All share the word "sky,"

But there are great differences.

The sky that is the hole in the eye of a needle,
The sky that is a steady eye,
The sky that appears in the hole,
The sky of colors and shapes,
And the sky that pervades the elements:
These are to be linked up with the doors to the vehicles.

Everything appears within the five elements,
So when outer appearances are destroyed,
Inner appearances are also destroyed.

There are two true foundations for the secret elements.
These are also two kinds of real things:
Entities of delusion,
And entities in our philosophical theories.

Entities of delusion are either external or internal.

The destruction of the five elements
Will be when the seven fires of karma,
The one of water,
And the last wind
Make it that way.

In the end,
We rest in emptiness.
When the private winds of spontaneous realization
Do not blow,
We do not even have a name
For what happens within them.

We do not even have a name
For the compassion of the Buddha!

We do not even have a name
For the samsara of sentient beings!

The four winds are mighty over all,
And are the strength of our doors.
Our own discomforts, losses, attachments,
Our place and its emptiness,

Are also like that.

The time that they are present is comprehensive.
From out of the great and inexhaustible treasury
Of the foundation of all things
Everything will be in the womb of Brahma,
And everyone will work on their attachments within it.

If we do not cut through the roots of this attachment
It will be extremely difficult to break out from
The pits of samsara.

The cause of the great elements
Is the one.

This is a great vision,
A great clarity.
This is not an idea.
It is spontaneously realized.
It is the ancestor of the three times.

If we do not cut through
This ancestor of ancestors
At the roots,
It will not be possible to break out from
The pits of samsara.

This is the mountain that unites the three kinds of existence.[83]

O You who Know All Glory and Endowment,
Tara of Wisdom,
I praise you!

You are the guardian of living things.
Your essence is spontaneously realized.
We are connected,
While you are a precious jewel
That has no connections.

You are the presiding leader
Of those who dwell within the three times.

---

[83] Below the earth, on the earth, and in the sky.

You are the foundation of all things,
The ancestor of ancestors,
The Great One.
I respectfully bow to you,
And offer you praise.

These are the instructions that were given by our teacher.

From the Tantra on the Non-duality of the God and the Demons, this is chapter eighteen: Living in a Peaceful Abiding.

TEACHINGS ON THE ROOTS
OF OUR ATTACHMENTS TO THE WORLD

Then again the most pure one exclaimed:

Vajra Dharma Mati,
Listen!

This is not empty!
It is the foundation of all things!

I will teach you how we are attached to it.

From the first,
None of us who make up the primary entourage
Were foretold of in the foundation.
During the interim,
We have been deluded within the roots of samsara.
In the end,
We will attain the fruition of self-liberation.

The king of self-liberation is the eye of wisdom.
We see with this eye,
But to the eye that is shadowed
This will not be clear.

He who holds the treasury of omniscient wisdom
Is a master,

A Tantra of the Great Perfection

One who has the power of a wisdom that is knowledge.

I will explain this to you.
You must listen in a respectful manner.

Without limiting any vastness,
Or falling into any bias,
There is a greatness that is spontaneously formed.
Those who live are attached to this.

The world has arisen from a union.
This is the root of the five great ones.
Their function is to emerge as the three kinds of existence.

The world has three kinds of root-nerves[84] to its foundation.
The three aspects of this foundation are brought together at the core.
The three kinds of roots are dear to us
When we are on a path,
For from them there emerges
The three kinds of bardo,
And from them there emerge
The three kinds of summit.
Their fruition is to cut through everything.
These are the five summits that are to be cut through,
The three roots,
And the one bardo.

The great one of the light,[85]
Who will wipe away the world,
Is at the border where compassion dawns.

On the path,
The people are divided into two.
There are these three: Tigers, lions, and bears.
These three are considered to be the greatest
By those on the causal path.
I teach them about the ways they are attached to their existences.

Existence is possible in three ways:
Outer, inner, and secret.

---

[84] rTsa
[85] 'Od po che

They come from a solitary union.[86]

So he spoke.

From the Tantra on the Non-duality of the Gods and the Demons, this is chapter nineteen: Teachings on the Roots of our Attachments to the World.

---

[86] sByor ba'i dgon pa

ATTACHMENT TO THE LAND OF THE GODS AND TEACHING THE DHARMA THERE

Then again the most pure one exclaimed:

Vajra Dharma Mati,
Listen!

Sarvva Karmma Loka Kuru Abhiṣeka Abhidha |

Thus did he present the word.

All things are good works.
They do not stop,
So it is possible that the world is a real entity.
When we do not understand the unborn
We will not be aware of our own abilities.

Loka Sarvvacchadana |

A time in which we will be free
From the abode of samsara
Does not exist.

You,
Listen to this well
In your mind!

A Tantra of the Great Perfection

I will teach you about the destruction of our inner attachments.

There is the base, the entity, and what is between them.
We assume that these three are not the same thing.
This is how we are attached to differences.
It is possible that they come from a solitary union.

At first,
There is the self-evident Sambhogakāya.
It is just when we partake of the pleasure there is in this
That we become beings of consciousness.
Our feelings and conceptions become small.

When we do not understand that the light that appears to us
Is self-evident,
We become attached to it,
And the nets of this world
Fall upon us.

We become connected to a single white and red seed,[87]
And the nets of magical illusion are truly upon us.

Through these connections things clarify in our eyes.
The two of them are of one substance with the sun and the moon.
They are lamps for the dark arteries[88] of the urṇākośa.[89]

The brain is called "a full conch."
The nerves are present in the manner of a parasol.
This is the fine home of Vijaya.
From there,
In the great bliss at the crowns of our heads,
There appear our four root heads:
Two for ambrosia,
And two for the sciences.[90]

In our hands there rest four vajras.
In the fine home of Vijaya,
On thirty-two root petals,

---

[87] Thig le
[88] Nag phra
[89] This is the area between and just above the eyebrows.
[90] gTsug lag

Dwell the thirty two who are truly empowered.

The mightiest of the gods Śakra,
Who is a Nirmaṇakāya,
Dwells there.

In the central nerve-knot at the navel,
The mightiest of the gods blazes in bliss.
Through his blessings,
The gods are dispersed all over.

It is through the blessings
Of the magnificent transmissions of the gods,[91]
That we may attain the siddhi of great bliss.

I will explain the seven kinds of jewels
As symbolic Dharmas.
The eyes, ears, nose, and tongue,
The lungs, heart, and the body:
These are the seven.

This describes our understanding of precious jewels.

From the Tantra on the Non-duality of the Gods and the Demons, this is chapter twenty: Attachment to the Land of the Gods and Teaching the Dharma There.

---

[91] Lha rgyud chen po

The Gods and the Demons Are Not Two

ATTACHMENT TO SELF-ORIGINATING COMPASSION WHILE IN THE LAND OF THE HUMANS

Then again the most pure one exclaimed:

Listen,
Vajra Dharma Mati,
You!

I will teach you the ways
We are attached to being human.

At the summit of the three nerves
There is a joining into three circles.[92]
The eight nerves are the eight islands.
The four nerves are the four continents.
The mountain at the center is our most excellent heart.
In the hollow of a crystal there is a wish-fulfilling tree.
Our hearts lust for the black iron mountains.

The seven mountains,
The seven valleys,
And the seven lakes:
We join them all together,
And become attached to them

---

[92] Thig le

As if they were a vessel.

When compassion falls from above
Our youthful strength is far away.
That which is helpful to our strength
Is not something we can taste.
Being proud about this,
We are attached to being human.

The caste of petty lords in their pride
Dwells in the South.
The caste of kings in its hatred
Dwells in the East.
The Brahmins who cleanse and bathe their desires
Are in the West.
The caste of the majority in their jealousies
Are in the North.
The Caṇḍas and Caṇḍālas
Are employed in all the bad jobs,
So they travel from their homes to go everywhere.

There is a circle in the middle of them all.
The Blessed One Śākyamuni appears there
And dwells among these five castes.
This is described in the Root Tantra,
But I will explain it once again.

Then he exclaimed:

Sarvva Prajñā Jñāna Upadeśa Krama Guhya Eka Tila Prasara Kala Dhuha |

The unerring stages in the upadeśa instructions
Use brilliant knowledge and wisdom in all things.
If someone does not understand the secret significance,
We will teach them that the unified circle is complicated.

Even though we complicate it,
There is only one thing.

So he spoke.

From the Tantra on the Non-duality of the Gods and the Demons, this is chapter twenty-one: Attachment to Self-Originating Compassion while in the Land of the Humans.

THE WAYS IN WHICH
THE ASURAS ARE ATTACHED
AND TURNING THE WHEEL OF THE DHARMA
FOR THEM

Then the most pure one exclaimed:

Listen,
Vajra Dharma Mati,
You!

I will teach you the ways we are attached
To what is neither divine nor human.

Our attachment to the life-nerve[93] within our hearts
Results in a great bliss ripening at the crown of our head.
Its petals are like those of a lotus.

On the sixteen great nerves at our throats,
There are the sixteen who are neither divine nor human:
Light and True Light,
Appearance and Luminous Appearance,
Blessings, Happiness, and Joy in Quarreling,
The Quarrel Maker, and the one Free From Quarreling,
The Bearer of Merit, the Keeper of Bliss,
And the Guardian of the Good,

---

[93] Srog rtsa

A Tantra of the Great Perfection

The One with a Net, and the Net-Light.
The View of the Sun, and the Light that Has no Sun.

They abide in an effulgence
That is like a tree.

Then again compassion descended from above
And the king of the Asuras Vemacitra,
Who was overcome by wrath in his war with the gods,
Turned the wheel of the five compassionate poisons
For them.

This is the Great Tantra on the Revolt of the Asura Armies.[94]
It cuts through the four nerves of wrath at their roots.
It teaches that the gods' own light
Is like the sun.
It turns the wheel of the self-originating Dharma.
It shares the taste of being an elemental spirit.
It liberates our attachments and hatreds.

In sharing the taste of our weapons,
We blaze in bliss.
In sharing the taste of our armor
We are blazing jewels.
In sharing the taste of our sorrow,
Its self-liberation dawns on us.
In sharing the taste of our battles and wars,
They will turn out to be embodiments of the Dharma.
In sharing the taste of fruit from the trees,
They will turn out to be ambrosia.

Great bliss,
The space of the Dharma and of self-originating wisdom,
Will dawn upon us.

This is not *Sarvva Loka*.

Karma Kuru Dhātu Jñāna Eka Tila Ratna Dai Cakra Mahā Dhathim |

---

[94] Lha ma yin gyul ngo bzlog pa'i rgyud chen po. This is the Title of a Tantra that is also preserved in the rNying ma rgyud 'bum. In the mTshams brag manuscript edition it is in volume 4 on pages 632-682. In the gTing skyes edition it is in volume 4 on pages 434-471.

When everything in the world is self-evident,
The good works of the Asuras will be completed.
Our dominion and our wisdom are not two things.
The unified circle is apparent to us.
The blazing jewel light is there within us.
Through the compassion of the Dharma Wheel,
We have been taught equanimity,
And now everything is melting into the dominion of the Dharma.

So he spoke.

From the Tantra on the Non-duality of the Gods and the Demons, this is chapter twenty-two: The Ways in which the Asuras are Attached and Turning the Wheel of the Dharma for Them.

The Gods and the Demons Are Not Two

THE WAYS WE ARE ATTACHED TO THE WORLD OF THE ANIMALS AND THE DESCENT OF COMPASSION EVEN ON THEM

Then the most pure one exclaimed:

Listen,
Vajra Dharma Mati,
You!

I will teach you the ways we are
Attached to being animals.

Here again,
We descend from above into the three nerves,
Then into sixty four places that are not to be predicted.
Something that is unpredictable is at the root of our birth.

Whether we will be born from a womb,
Born by caesarian section,[95]
Miraculously born,
Egg born,
Or born from heat and moisture,
And which place, what karma, with which food, and which body:
All of these things are not predictable.

---

[95] gZhogs skyes

A Tantra of the Great Perfection

Then in the circle that is at the center of them all
There appears Most Firm,[96]
The lion over the animals.

The wheel of the Dharma of compassion is predictable,
And it is taught on the four continents.
The doors that are not predictable
Are described as being doors that have been predicted.

The predictions about ignorance are that it is the Dharmakāya.
Predictions about our place of birth
Are experiences of wisdom as it rises up in us.
Predictions of a result are our vajra embodiments.
Predictions of karma are the practices of self-originating wisdom.
Predictions about food devour the apparent world as their food.
The prediction about our bodies
Is that our body is a clarity that fills the sky.

Then he exclaimed:

Sarvva Bītta Mula Tiwa Vajra He Guhya Ratna Phala Tantra Dharmma Ratna | Cakṣu Tiryaka Jñāna Cakra Phala Mahā Bodhisvāta Svabhāwa Viśudha Jñāna Kaya A |

Everything is self-evident ignorance for them.
The ignorance of the animals
Is a great stupidity,
But the teachings on the vajra body
Are a delight!

Great secrets are like good jewels.
Once we have understood
The significance of the Tantra's reality,
We use it to open our eyes to precious jewels,
And we turn the wheel of wisdom for the animals.

The Good One is an embodiment of self-originating enlightenment.
He is a great Bodhisattva.
His stainless purity is his embodiment of wisdom.
His being unborn is his embodiment of eternity.

---

[96] Rab brtan

So he spoke.

From the Tantra on the Non-duality of the Gods and the Demons, this is chapter twenty-three: The Ways we are Attached to the World of the Animals and the Descent of Compassion Even on Them.

TEACHINGS TO DESTROY
THE HUNGRY GHOSTS' ATTACHMENT
TO THE EXTERNAL WORLD
AND
TURNING THE WHEEL
THAT BRINGS COMPASSION
DOWN FROM ABOVE

Then the most pure one exclaimed:

Vajra Dharma Mati,
Listen!

I will teach you about the way we are attached
To life as hungry ghosts.

You must listen with a one-pointed mind!

We are working to cut off the summit
From the three primary nerves.
These three nerves are attached together in our private parts.[97]
There are external and internal obstructions,
And there are those who have these obstructions.

These are the hungry ghosts.
They are the elementals that move through the sky,
The hungry ghosts whose karma has fully ripened,
The hungry ghosts who support those who reside there,
And the hungry ghosts who have realized their own results.

---

[97] gSang ba'i gnas

Their numbers are inconceivable!
They transcend our thoughts!

Compassion descends from above,
And the Sage:
Queen Burning Mouth[98]
Purifies our three nerves.

When we recognize this
Our external obstructions will be removed.
When we recognize that these three things
Are synchronously born,
This will remove our internal obstructions.

When we recognize these three self-liberations,
This will remove both external and internal obstructions.
This has no location.
It is a magnificent self-appearance.

They move around in the sky without direction.
When we recognize that they are a magnificent clear light,
We attain the magnificent result of being self-liberated.

We remain in our bodies,
And we move in our breath.

The demonic hungry ghosts who continue to live here
Will recognize that there is nothing real about their flickering,
And the hungry ghosts that are staying around
Will be liberated into their own place.

All of our karmas are made from flickerings.
Our understandings are made from wisdom.
Our lack of understanding is made from ignorance.
These two are similar in their functions,
But they are not the same entity.

The fully matured hungry ghosts
And the full maturation of our results
Are similar in that they are results,
But there is a great difference.

---

[98] Kha 'bar rgyal mo

The Gods and the Demons Are Not Two

Fully matured results reach to the end,
So a reality that has no location
Will dawn upon our understanding.

So he spoke.

Then he taught us these words:

Sarvva Loka Pretaka Karmma Kuru Jñāna Guhya Ratna Cakṣu |
Pariśuddha Ā |

Everything is samsara for a hungry ghost,
But their good works will be quickly completed.
They will teach a secret wisdom to themselves,
And open up the magnificent eye that is a precious jewel.
As they work to remove every obstruction,
The Dharmakāya will become visible.

So he spoke.

From the Tantra on the Non-duality of the Gods and the Demons, this is chapter twenty-four: Teachings to Destroy the Hungry Ghosts' Attachment to the External World and Turning the Wheel that Brings Compassion Down from Above.

The Gods and the Demons Are Not Two

TURNING THE WHEEL
OF THE DHARMA OF COMPASSION
IN THE ABODES OF HELL

Then the most pure one exclaimed:

Listen,
Vajra Dharma Mati,
You!

I will teach you about the ways
We become attached to life in hell.

At the first there are the three nerves,
But the nerve for the soul[99] that is at the tip becomes black.
It turns counterclockwise in a mandala of fire.
It has the character of the eight nerves on the soles of our feet
And we become attached to life in the eight hot hells.

At the center of them all
There appears the compassionate Ox-headed Awa.
His A is a garland of blazing volcanoes.

Then he exclaimed these words:

Narakka Agne Jala Prajñā Pāramita Hrida Jñāna Mahā Dhātu Ā |

The eight hot hells have liberated themselves from being

---

[99] bLar rtsa

A self-originating place to be,
And instead of the blazing fire-tongues of hell,
We use wisdom to clear out our hearts.

Within the dominion of great wisdom
Nothing is born.

That is the meaning of what he said.

From the Tantra on the Non-duality of the Gods and the Demons, this is chapter twenty-five: Turning the Wheel of the Dharma of Compassion in the Abodes of Hell.

TURNING THE WHEEL
OF SELF-EVIDENT COMPASSION
FOR THE COLD HELLS
AND FOR THE TEMPORARY HELLS
THAT ARE NEAR THEM

Then the most pure one exclaimed:

Listen,
Vajra Dharma Mati,
You!

I will teach you about the ways
We become attached to life in the cold hells.

At first there are the three nerves,
Then there is a clockwise turning mandala of water
In the place of the lotus,
The eight nerves at the soles of our feet,
Those with the character of the moon and the sun.
The nerves that are within them manifest as wheels of water.
The eight cold hells appear from them.

Now descending from above,
To turn the wheel of the Dharma of compassion
From out of the three nerves,
There is the one called King of Dharma.

It is because he is a king of the Dharma of compassion

That he is called a Dharma King,
And he teaches as an embodiment of the Dharma of peace
Even in the mandalas of the cold water.

Then he taught us these words:

Naga Raca Manu Preta Kayanne Prajñā Pāramitā Hridaya |

The meaning of this is:

Primary among the Sages
Is the King of Hell.
For beings who are hungry ghosts,
It is the King of the Dharma.
They must abide within a heart of wisdom.

So he spoke.

I bow to the Redactor of Brilliant Knowledge and Wisdom,
The protector of we who live!

The great King of the Dharma said these things:

The cold hells are embodiments of wisdom.
The self-liberation of hell is pervasive within its own circle.

So he spoke.

The temporary hells that surround them
Are our two heels becoming attached to life there.
Both of them get turned around,
So they are temporary.

The Sage has taught us about non-duality.
This is what will liberate those in the temporary hells
Into their own places.

So he spoke.

From the Tantra on the Non-duality of the Gods and the Demons, this is chapter twenty-six: Turning the Wheel of Self-evident Compassion for the Cold Hells and for the Temporary Hells that are Near Them.

TEACHING THE WAY WE BECOME ATTACHED TO THE VAJRA HELL AND TURNING THE WHEEL OF THE DHARMA OF COMPASSION THERE

Then the most pure one exclaimed:

Listen,
Vajra Dharma Mati,
You!

I will teach you about the ways
We are attached to the vajra hell!

At first,
From out of our three nerves,
In the nerve of the vajra vase,
The three nerves manifest in the shape of vajras.
This is the support structure for the vajra hell.

Compassion descends upon it,
Yet a vajra body is not a compounded thing.
The things that draw us into the vajra hell
Are the things we like and our greatest joys.

There are the synchronously born delights,
And there is the embodiment of the Sage,
Who is free from these delights.
This is described as being:
"The descent of compassion from above."

Garab Dorje is the Nirmaṇakāya.
He appeared to the seven sages,
And taught them to call him: "Garab Dorje."[100]

The Nirmaṇakāya Garab Dorje
Appears on the path of the nerve of compassion.
The Sambhogakāya Vajrasattva
Appears on the path of the essential nerve of clear light.
The Dharmakāya, the All Good One,
Appears on the path of the nerve of wisdom.
When these three are combined into one
It is called: "*Awadhuti.*"

A is the unborn, the All Good One.
Wa is the five bodies and the five wisdoms,
And is also called: "Vajra Akṣobhya."
Dhuti is the Nirmaṇakāya, the source of compassion.

The Nirmaṇakāya is Garab Dorje.
It is because he unites the three bodies that he is Dorje, a vajra.
A vajra body is not a compounded thing.

The vajra that is a mark upon our bodies
Is a sign that the three bodies are present within us.
When we recognize our inner potency,
There will be signs that the three bodies are manifest within us.
When we recognize their secret significance
The compassion of the three bodies will be our portion.

I am teaching you here
To recognize the self-liberation
Of those who are in the vajra hell.

Then he exclaimed this forcefully:

Nagara Vajra Ajñāṇa Tila Mula Mahā |
Krika Pradu Asi |

This is what it means:

---

[100] dGa' rab rdo rje. Literally, "Vajra of Supreme Delight."

The Gods and the Demons Are Not Two

The teaching that the vajra hell is unborn
Is a teaching on the recognition of self-liberation.
The Mahayana dawns on us
Without our looking for it.
This is the Nirmaṇakāya's great armor:
The dimension of the unborn
Melts into a single body.

So he spoke.

From the Tantra on the Non-duality of the Gods and the Demons, this is chapter twenty-seven: Teaching the Way We Become Attached to the Vajra Hell and Turning the Wheel of the Dharma of Compassion There.

A TEACHING THAT TURNS THE WHEEL OF THE DHARMA OF COMPASSION ON ATTACHMENT, DESTRUCTION, AND EMPTINESS, ALONG WITH THE THREE KINDS OF BEINGS WHO EXPERIENCE THEM, AND THAT THEIR MAGNIFICENT PILGRIMAGE SITES WILL NOT ENDURE

Then the most pure one exclaimed:

Listen,
Vajra Dharma Mati,
You!

The blessings of compassion descend from above.
It is in consideration of these three that they appear:
The path, the place, and the person.

When the descent of compassion from above happens,
We are attached to an above and a below in this world.

These five: The sky, wind, water, fire, and earth
Self-evidently descend from above
And become attached to what is external.
If it were not for this core of external elements
The compassion of the Sambhogakāya would not manifest.
This is also the descent of compassion.

A Tantra of the Great Perfection

It if were not for the core of the five internal elements
The compassion of the Dharmakāya would have no place to appear.
This is also the descent of its compassion.

This is also the descent of the three secret nerves.
If it were not for the core of these three secret nerves
The spontaneously born triad would have no place to appear.

If it were not for the vital core of these three nerves,
The Vajra Dharmakāya would have no place to appear.
This is also the descent of compassion.

If it were not for the core of connectedness among the nerves,
The transmission of the meaning would have nowhere to appear.
This is also the descent of compassion.

If we do not bring our senses into one,
We will have no method to bring forth
The transmission of the upadeśa instructions.
This is also the descent of compassion.

If we do not understand that the nerves are self-originating,
We will have no method to elicit the core of the upadeśa instructions.
This is also the decent of compassion.

If it were not for the core of distorted eyes[101] among the nerves,
The Tantra, transmission, and upadeśa instructions
Would lose their roots.
This is also the descent of compassion.

If it were not for the core in which the three nerves are one.
There would be no way to bring forth a unified circle.
This is also the descent of compassion.

If it were not for the core of being alone and self-liberated,
There would be no self-liberation of the base, path, and fruit.
This is also the descent of compassion.

Compassion descends up and down through all things,
An analogy is that there are clouds in the sky and the rain falls.

---

[101] 'Khrul mig

Then he exclaimed this:

Sūrya Candra Agne Sane Ratna Jñāna Guhye Mahā Dharmā Dhātu Bhidha Mahā Mūla Samayā Vajra Kāya | Tila Eka A |

The fire of the sun is a symbol for wisdom.
The water of the moon is a symbol for methods.
This is the level where wisdom and methods are a jewel rosary.
This is the magnificent secret wisdom.

Our dominion of the Dharma is the wisdom we are aware of.
This is the significance of the Mahayana.
It must be taught to those who have samaya.

A vajra body is not a compounded thing.
The three bodies are a unified circle.
This is a description of the unborn.

So he spoke.

From the Tantra on the Non-duality of the Gods and the Demons, this is chapter twenty-eight: A Teaching that Turns the Wheel of the Dharma of Compassion on Attachment, Destruction, and Emptiness, along with the Three Kinds of Beings who Experience Them, and That Their Magnificent Pilgrimage Sites[102] Will Not Endure.

---

[102] gNas chen

TEACHING THAT COMPASSION FALLS UPON THE PHILOSOPHICAL THEORIES IN THE SCRIPTURES ABOUT THE VEHICLES AND ON THEIR CONCLUSIVE RESULT

Then the most pure one exclaimed:

Listen,
Vajra Dharma Mati,
You!

The designated visions
That are the philosophical theories of the vehicles,
And the self-liberating philosophical theories that are not Dharmas
Are both to be understood as being either biased or unbiased.
These two kinds of understanding share the sound of being paths,
But there is a great difference.

Philosophical theories about the base that are biased understandings,
And unbiased and spontaneously realized understandings
Both share the word "understanding,"
But there is a great difference.

Philosophical theories that have biased understandings of results
And unbiased understandings in which defining marks are set free
Both share the word "understanding,"
But there is a great difference.

A Tantra of the Great Perfection

Precious things such as gold
And a perfect store of precious gems
Share the word "precious,"
But there is a great difference.

The truths of the vehicles and for sentient beings
And the great perfection in which we delude our own sentience
Both share the word "sentience,"
But there is a great difference.

The truth of minute atoms for the Auditors
And the illusion of minute atoms for the Private Buddhas
Both share the words "minute atom,"
But there is a great difference.

The non-duality of our dominion and our wisdom in the Anu
And the non-duality of the self-evident great perfection
Both share the word "non-duality,"
But there is a great difference.

The dawn of the light-bearing *Candra*
And the dawn of the light-bearing *Surya*
Both share the word "dawn,"
But there is a great difference.

The gathering of our two accumulations into completion
And the magnificent self-completion of our two accumulations
Share the word "accumulations,"
But there is a great difference.

Then he exclaimed these words:

Mahā Mula Tila Eka Prasara Sadru Kala Pañca Dharaṃ |
Samaya Mahā Mula A Si A |

The meaning of this is:

It is the specific nature of the Mahayana
To complicate the unified circle.

To understand the meaning of non-duality
And to be a core of self-liberation,
All the five bodies must be formed into ourselves.

Know that this is the great samaya!
The unborn is to be realized within us!

So he spoke.

From the Tantra on the Non-duality of the Gods and the Demons, this is chapter twenty-nine: Teaching that Compassion Falls upon the Philosophical Theories in the Scriptures about the Vehicles and on their Conclusive Result.

THE SPIKE OF REASON IS PLANTED THROUGH THE EXTERNAL AND INTERNAL, WHICH PLANTS THE SPIKE OF ANALOGIES FOR TEACHING, PLANTS THE SPIKE OF WORDS OF VISION, AND PLANTS THE SPIKE OF MEANINGS INTO WORDS

Then the most pure one exclaimed:

Listen,
Vajra Dharma Mati,
You!

I will now teach you the recognition of the core.

The way to view the flashing
Is as an external spike.[103]
It is not necessary to recognize all the demons
Or to cling with our minds to designated visualizations.

The turning of the wheel of clear light
Is an instruction that describes an external viewpoint.
We use one method to see everything.
An analogy is that we see things perfectly and without confusion
In a house that is a brocade tent.

The upadeśa instructions for the single way of looking are dear.

---

[103] gZer

They cut through exaggerations
That claim that Dharmas have general and private definitions
By using a single way of seeing them!
An analogy is that this is like a reflection in a mirror.

We understand that everything is naturally pristine.
We see the six classes of living beings
With a single method of looking at them.

The general overlords and the wardens of the doors
For the six classes of living beings
Are like visions of the planets and the stars in the sky.
We understand how to sell the ground meat of our ignorance.
We use a single way of seeing to perceive the unified circle.

So he spoke.

From the Tantra on the Non-duality of the Gods and the Demons, this is chapter thirty: The Spike of Reason Is Planted through the External and Internal, which Plants the Spike of Analogies for Teaching, Plants the Spike of Words of Vision, and Plants the Spike of Meanings into Words.

REVEALING THE HEART
THAT CONCEALS
THE EXTERNAL, INTERNAL, AND SECRET

Then the most pure one exclaimed:

Listen,
Vajra Dharma Mati,
You!

I will explain the spikes[104] that are secret and that are most secret.

There are these three:
The six methods,
The analogy,
And its meaning.

The way that the secret is imparted is as a pure experience.
It is a circle of self-originating wisdom.
The unsurpassed great spike
Is a recognition of the spike that is in the analogy.
This is dear.

The connections among methods that use symbolic spikes are dear.
Through being taught a single symbol
All the meanings dawn on us.

---

[104] gZer

The symbolic spike is taught to be a sign.
Using this sign,
The meaning will dawn on us.

So he spoke.

From the Tantra on the Non-duality of the Gods and the Demons, this is chapter thirty-one: Revealing the Heart that Conceals the External, Internal, and Secret.

THE BEQUEST OF THE TANTRA

Then the Blessed One,
The glorious All Good One,
Spoke to Vajra Dharma Mati:

This is the King of the Tantras for the great road of freedom.
Take it as the King of the Tantras that bless us.
It liberates the gods and the rākṣasa demons,
So we take it to be the Tantra
On the Non-duality of the Gods and the Demons.

Everything, with no exceptions,
Is complete within this,
So we take it to be a Tantra on the Circle that Subsumes All Things.[105]

So he spoke.

Vajra Dharma Mati and the dakini Sun Lion were overjoyed.

From the Tantra on the Non-duality of the Gods and the Demons this is chapter thirty-two: The Bequest of the Tantra.

This Tantra that goes beyond the Dharma is finished.

Mangalaṃ

---

[105] Kun 'dus thig le'i rgyud

A Tantra of the Great Perfection

THE TIBETAN TEXT

Images from the rNying ma rgyud 'bum mTshams brag dgon kyi bri ma, National Library, Royal Government of Bhutan, Thimpu, 1982. 46 Vols. Volume 17, pp. 783-873.

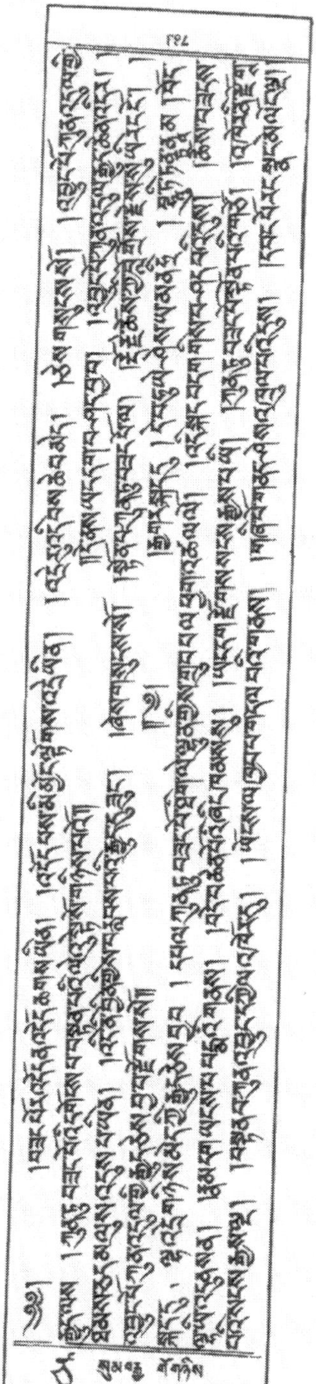

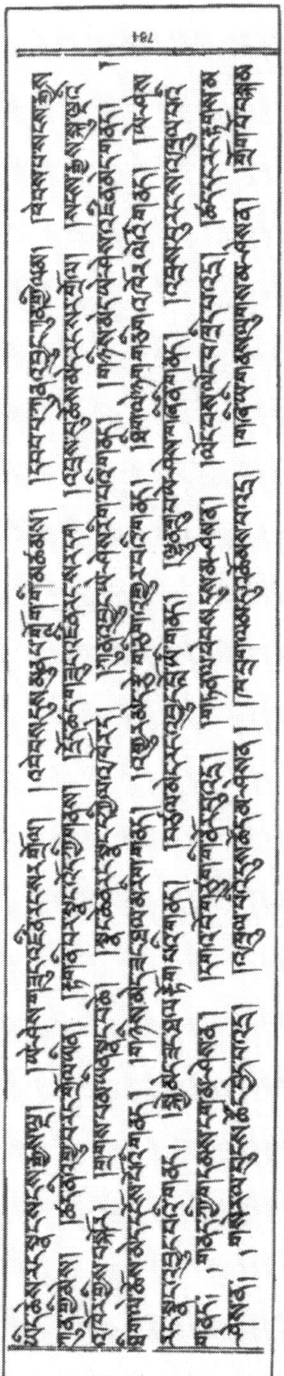

The Gods and the Demons Are Not Two

A Tantra of the Great Perfection

The Gods and the Demons Are Not Two

A Tantra of the Great Perfection

The Gods and the Demons Are Not Two

A Tantra of the Great Perfection

The Gods and the Demons Are Not Two

A Tantra of the Great Perfection

The Gods and the Demons Are Not Two

A Tantra of the Great Perfection

The Gods and the Demons Are Not Two

A Tantra of the Great Perfection

The Gods and the Demons Are Not Two

A Tantra of the Great Perfection

The Gods and the Demons Are Not Two

A Tantra of the Great Perfection

The Gods and the Demons Are Not Two

A Tantra of the Great Perfection

The Gods and the Demons Are Not Two

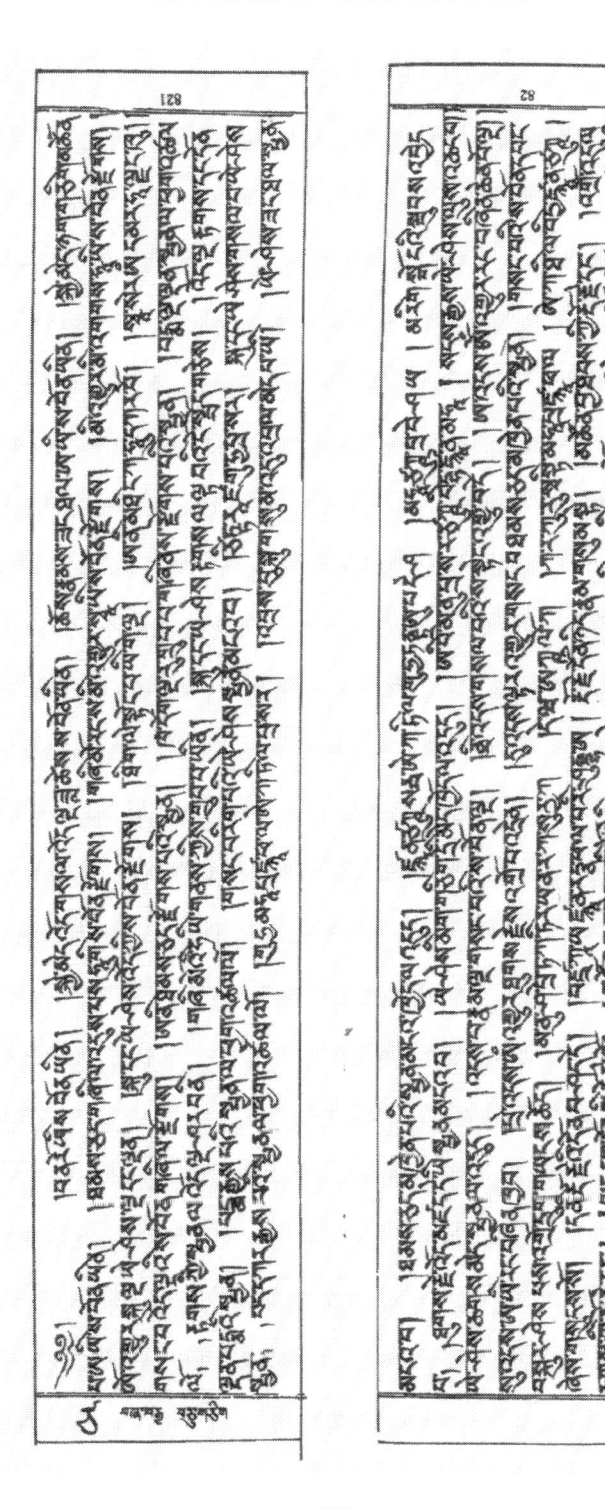

A Tantra of the Great Perfection

The Gods and the Demons Are Not Two

A Tantra of the Great Perfection

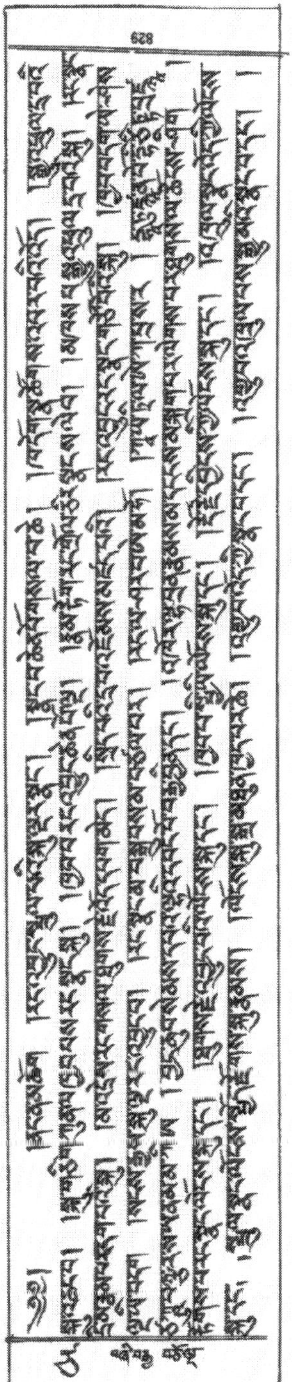

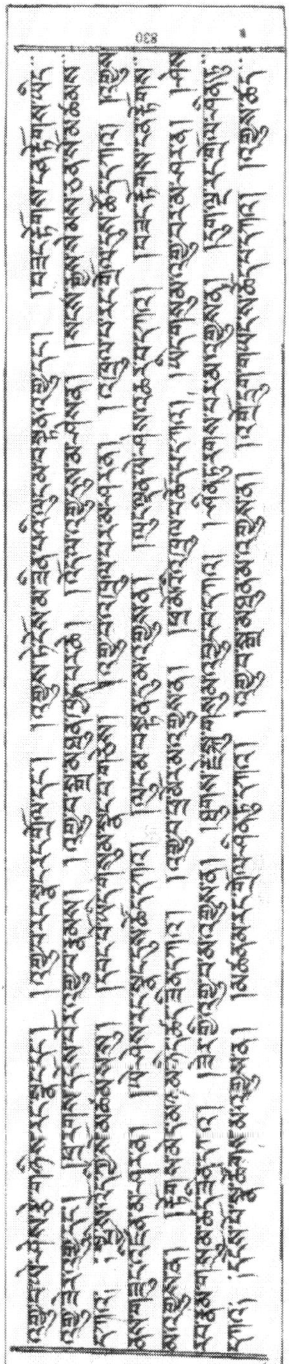

A Tantra of the Great Perfection

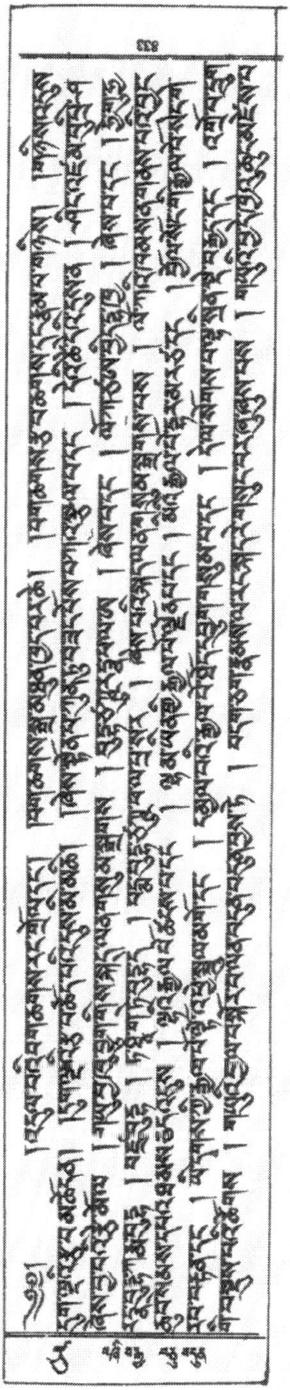

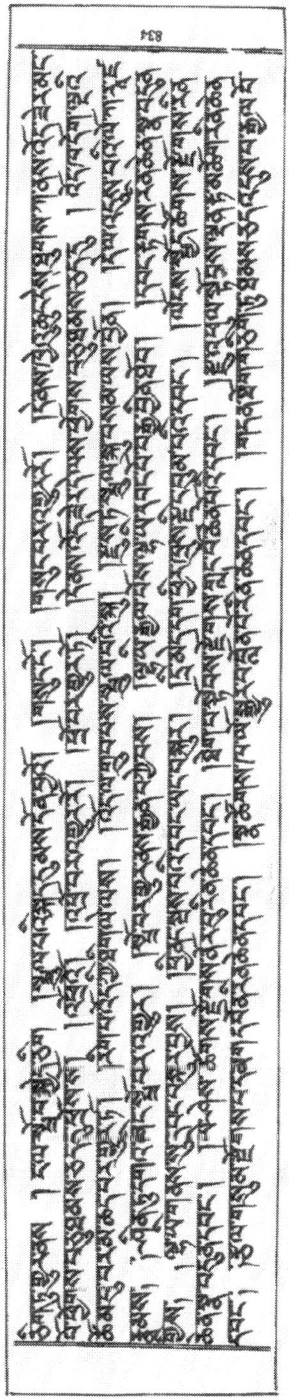

A Tantra of the Great Perfection

The Gods and the Demons Are Not Two

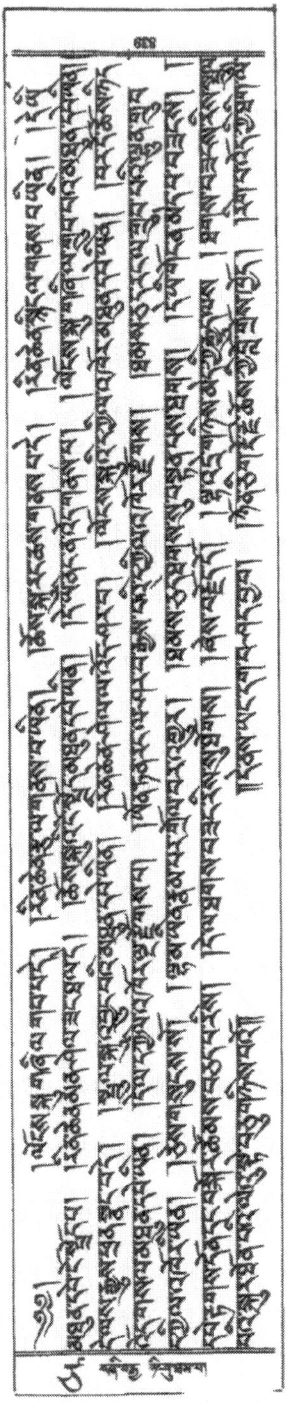

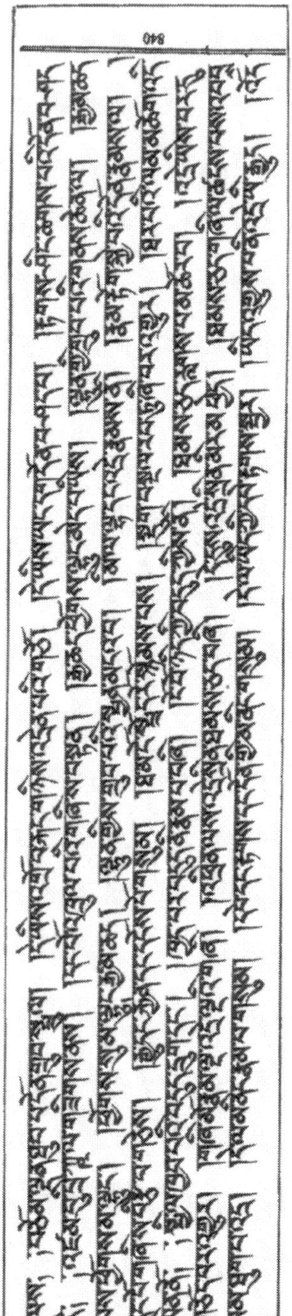

The Gods and the Demons Are Not Two

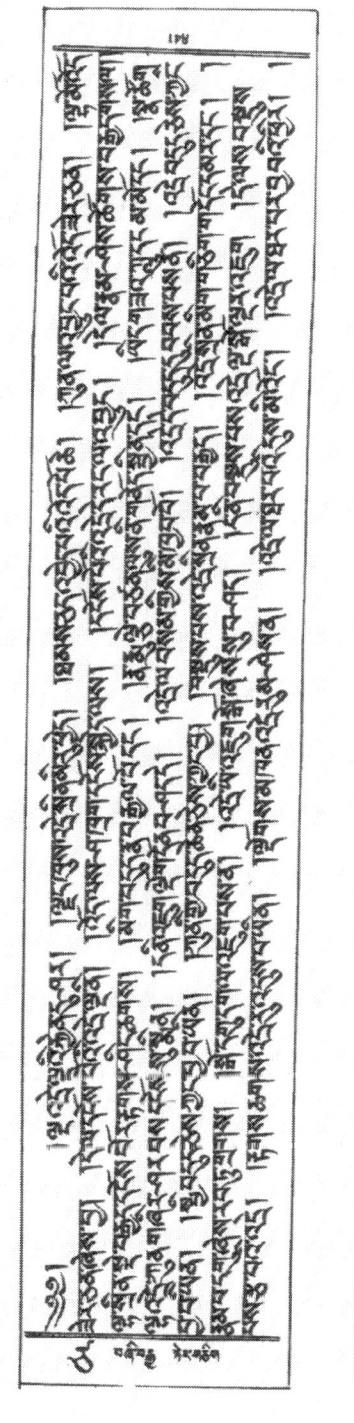

A Tantra of the Great Perfection

The Gods and the Demons Are Not Two

A Tantra of the Great Perfection

The Gods and the Demons Are Not Two

A Tantra of the Great Perfection

The Gods and the Demons Are Not Two

A Tantra of the Great Perfection

The Gods and the Demons Are Not Two

A Tantra of the Great Perfection

The Gods and the Demons Are Not Two

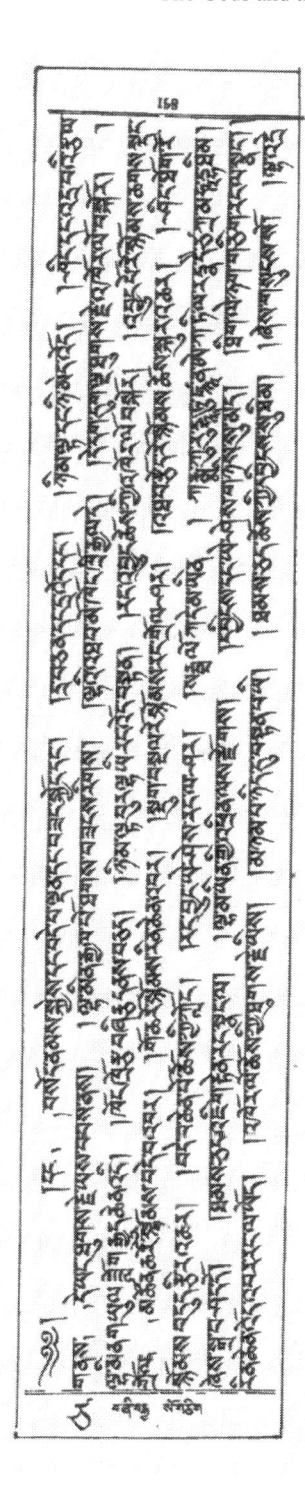

A Tantra of the Great Perfection

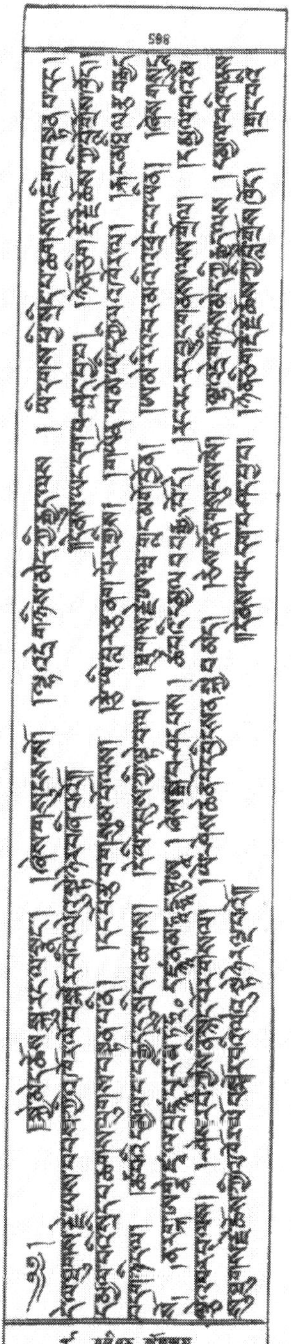

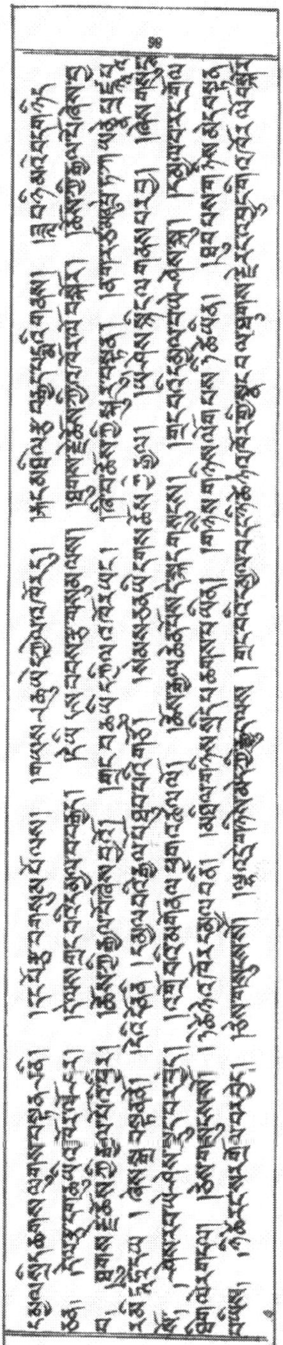

A Tantra of the Great Perfection

The Gods and the Demons Are Not Two

A Tantra of the Great Perfection

The Gods and the Demons Are Not Two

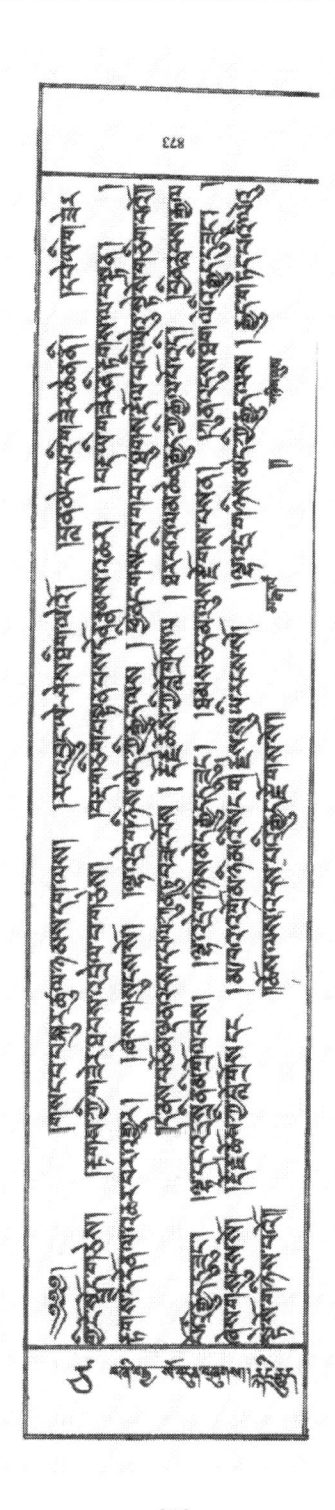

ABOUT THE TRANSLATOR

Christopher Wilkinson began his career in Buddhist literature at the age of fifteen, taking refuge vows from his guru Dezhung Rinpoche. In that same year he began formal study of Tibetan language at the University of Washington under Geshe Ngawang Nornang and Turrell Wylie. He became a Buddhist monk, for three years, at the age of eighteen, living in the home of Dezhung Rinpoche while he continued his studies at the University of Washington. He graduated in 1980 with a B.A. degree in Asian Languages and Literature and another B.A. degree in Comparative Religion (College Honors, Magna Cum Laude, Phi Beta Kappa). After a two year tour of Buddhist pilgrimage sites throughout Asia he worked in refugee resettlement programs for five years in Seattle, Washington. He then proceeded to the University of Calgary for an M.A. in Buddhist Studies where he wrote a groundbreaking thesis on the Yangti transmission of the Great Perfection tradition titled "Clear Meaning: Studies on a Thirteenth Century rDzog chen Tantra." He proceeded to work on a critical edition of the Sanskrit text of the 20,000 line Perfection of Wisdom in Berkeley, California, followed by an intensive study of Burmese language in Hawaii. In 1990 he began three years' service as a visiting professor in English Literature in Sulawesi, Indonesia, exploring the remnants of the ancient Sri Vijaya Empire there. He worked as a research fellow for the Shelly and Donald Rubin Foundation for several years, playing a part in the early development of the Rubin Museum of Art. In the years that followed he became a Research Fellow at the Centre de Recherches sur les Civilisations de l'Asie Orientale, Collège de France, and taught at the University of Calgary as an Adjunct Professor for five years. He has published several volumes of translations of Tibetan literature, and is currently engaged in further translations of classic Buddhist literature.

A Tantra of the Great Perfection

NOTES TO INTRODUCTION

[i] The Rgyud 'bum of Vairocana : A collection of Ancient Tantras and Esoteric Instructions compiled and translated by the 8th century Tibetan Master reproduced from the rare manuscript belonging to Tokden Rinpoche of Gangon by Tashi Y. Tashigangpa. Leh, Ladakh, 1971. 8 Volumes. Vol 7, pp. 1-95.

[ii] The Marvelous Primordial State: The Mejung Tantra; Translated by Elio Guarisco, Adriano Clemente, and Jim Valby with the Precious Help of Chogyal Namkhai Norbu. Shang Shung Publications. 2013.

[iii] rNying ma rgyud 'bum mTshams brag dgon kyi bri ma, National Library, Royal Government of Bhutan, Thimpu, 1982. 46 Vols. Volume 17, pp. 783-873.

[iv] Lha ma yin gyul ngo bzlog pa'i rgyud. In the mTshams brag manuscript edition rNying ma rgyud 'bum it is in volume 4 on pages 632-682. In the gTing skyes edition it is in volume 4 on pages 434-471.

[v] 'Byung po kun 'dul shes bya ba'i rgyud. In the mTshams brag ms. It is in volume 17 pp. 710-783. In the gTing skyes manuscript it is in volume 5, pp. 41-100.

Made in United States
Orlando, FL
21 June 2023